ISBN: 9781313201506

Published by:
HardPress Publishing
8345 NW 66TH ST #2561
MIAMI FL 33166-2626

Email: info@hardpress.net
Web: http://www.hardpress.net

Wason
BV3345
G79

CORNELL UNIVERSITY LIBRARY

THE
CHARLES WILLIAM WASON
COLLECTION ON CHINA
AND THE CHINESE

BORNEO

The Land of River and Palm

The original of this book is in
the Cornell University Library.

There are no known copyright restrictions in
the United States on the use of the text.

http://www.archive.org/details/cu31924023051133

Albert Hester. *Clapton, London, N.E.*

RIGHT REV. W. R. MOUNSEY, D.D.,
Bishop of Labuan and Sarawak. Consecrated 25th March, 1909.

BORNEO

The Land of River and Palm

By

EDA GREEN

Joint-Author of "By Lake and Forest"

WITH PREFACE BY

THE LORD BISHOP OF LABUAN AND SARAWAK

"'Tis not what man Does which exalts him
But what man Would do."—BROWNING

BORNEO MISSION ASSOCIATION

COPIES TO BE OBTAINED FROM

THE HON. SEC.

STAINFORTH HOUSE, CLAPTON COMMON, N.E.

OR

MISS EDA GREEN

1A SHEFFIELD TERRACE, KENSINGTON

Price 2/- net

Wac...
BV3345
G79

w.67566

Dedicated

TO THE MEMORY OF

RAJAH BROOKE AND BISHOP McDOUGALL

PIONEERS AND FOUNDERS

OF

CHURCH AND STATE

PREFACE.

THE condition of the Diocese of Labuan and Sarawak at the present time is due largely to the lack of men. Until we have a very large increase in our European staff I can see little or no hope of advance.

Why do men not come to Borneo?

I think we shall find that few people know much about us or our history, and consequently we are not mentioned much in missionary circles.

My predecessors have been content to work on here, making few visits to England, hoping that their cry for help would sooner or later meet with a response which, alas! has not come.

Men did not come because amid the loud cries from other fields they did not hear the call from this Land of River and Palm. Neither men nor money were forthcoming because people did not know.

I am full of gratitude, therefore, to Miss Eda Green for writing this little book about us and our wonderful country, that men and women at home may have some accurate account of us and of our needs, and may be moved to help us. The proofs have been read in Borneo by those who know the country, and we are all astonished that such a vivid and accurate picture should have been drawn by one who has never been here.

I commend this book then to all who are keen to extend the Kingdom of God in the dark places of the earth.

W. ROBT. MOUNSEY,
Bishop of Labuan and Sarawak.

KUCHING, SARAWAK,
  30th *August*, 1909.

AUTHOR'S PREFATORY NOTE.

THE aim of this little book will be reached if it may be the means of stirring in any hearts the wish to do something to help the work in the Diocese of Labuan and Sarawak.

It is divided into eight chapters, with questions after each, and at the end of the book are some outline thoughts, in case it should be taken up by any class of readers studying the work of the Church in Borneo, but it makes no pretension to be a Study Circle Book, and is brought out in no connection whatever with the exhaustive books prepared by trained experts and published under the auspices of the Young People's Missionary Movement.

I wish to express my thanks to Dr. Hose, the late Bishop, to Archdeacon Sharp and to Mrs. Dexter Allen, for going through the MSS. and giving me the benefit of their corrections ; also to acknowledge my indebtedness to Mr. Ling Roth for much information taken from his *Natives of Sarawak*, and to the Rev. W. Howell.

AUTHOR'S PREFATORY NOTE

My sincere thanks are offered to His Highness the Rajah for permission to use his photograph and to Mrs. Bunyon for allowing me to have a hitherto unprinted portrait of Mrs. McDougall; also, for giving me the use of their copyright photographs, to the editor of S.P.G., to Miss Bunyon, to the British North Borneo Co., Messrs. Bassano, Messrs. Elliot & Fry, Mr. Albert Hester and *The Illustrated London News*.

To Dr. Charles Hose I owe much gratitude for his great kindness in permitting me to use his valuable photographs, and also to Mr. Ling Roth for most generously lending me many of his blocks, and for letting me reproduce his tribal map.

Other illustrations are from photographs taken by Mr. Hewitt, late Curator of the Sarawak Museum, and the late Mr. Gregg, Headmaster of S. Thomas' School, Kuching.

Those mentioned, and many unmentioned friends who by their help in various ways have made it possible to complete this book, I thank most sincerely, knowing that the wish of one and all has been to render service to a forlorn outpost, and to aid, if our joint work may in any way be so used, the building up of the KINGDOM OF GOD in Borneo.

E. EDA GREEN.

N.B.—The name of the Diocese should be pronounced Labūan and Sarāwak.

CONTENTS

	PAGE
PREFACE	vii
PREFATORY NOTE	ix

CHAP.
I. BORNEO AND ITS RICHES	1
II. THE PEOPLE AND THEIR CUSTOMS	21
III. THE PEOPLE, FEUDS, WAR, AND DEATH	47
IV. SUPERSTITIONS AND BELIEFS AND THEIR EFFECTS	66
V. HISTORY	86
VI. SIXTY YEARS OF MISSIONS	104
VII. POSITION OF THE CHURCH IN BORNEO NOW	125
VIII. RESPONSE OF THE CHURCH AT HOME	141
OUTLINE THOUGHTS	161
NAMES OF CLERGY AND LAY WORKERS	164
LIST OF MISSIONS	166
BORNEO MISSION ASSOCIATION	167

LIST OF ILLUSTRATIONS

PORTRAIT OF BISHOP MOUNSEY. Photo., Albert Hester
Frontispiece

	TO FACE PAGE
MAP OF BORNEO AND ITS SURROUNDINGS. Mr. Ling Roth	1
MAP OF THE DIOCESE OF LABUAN AND SARAWAK	3
COCOANUT GROVE. Mr. Hewitt	6
SAPONG RUBBER ESTATE. British North Borneo Co.	8
RAPID ON PARAN RIVER. Dr. C. Hose	10
MAIAS. Mr. Hewitt	10
KAYANS COLLECTING GUTTA-PERCHA. Dr. C. Hose	18
SEA-DYAK LONG HOUSE. Mr. Ling Roth (Mr. Hornaday)	22
PLAN OF SEA-DYAK LONG HOUSE. Mr. Ling Roth (Mr. Crosland)	24
BRIDGE	32
TRAVELLER'S PALMS. Mr. Hewitt	32
TEETH, TATTOED HANDS. Mr. Ling Roth	34
GIRL WEAVING. Dr. C. Hose	36
DYAKS WITH SEAT MATS	38
DUSUN LOOM. Mr. Ling Roth	42
DYAK CHIEF WITH HEADS. Dr. C. Hose	48
MODEL OF DYAK DUGOUT. Mr. Ling Roth (Mr. Leggatt)	50

xiv   LIST OF ILLUSTRATIONS

	TO FACE PAGE
SHIELDS. Mr. Ling Roth	52
PARANG QUIVER. Mr. Ling Roth	54
MAKING POISON FOR DARTS. Dr. C. Hose	56
SUMPITAN, CHARMS, JAR. Mr. Ling Roth	58
MILANAU GRAVE. Mr. Hewitt	60
SALONG, KLIERING, FIREDRILL. Mr. Ling Roth	62
MILANAU SORCERER. S.P.G.	70
KANOWIT. Mr. Ling Roth	74
KAYANS IN WAR DRESS. S.P.G.	76
WEAVING PATTERN, HORNBILL, BASKET. Mr. Ling Roth	78
OFFERINGS TO OMEN BIRDS. Dr. C. Hose	82
JUNGLE PATH. S.P.G.	82
SIR JAMES BROOKE. *Illustrated London News*	88
THE ASTANA	90
DYAKS IN FULL DRESS. S.P.G.	92
SEA-DYAK WOMAN	96
SIR CHARLES BROOKE, G.C.M.G. Photo., Bassano	100
PADAS RIVER. British North Borneo Co.	102
BISHOP MCDOUGALL	104
MRS. MCDOUGALL. By permission of Mrs. Bunyon	104
FONT. By permission of Miss Bunyon	108
ORCHID. Mr. Hewitt	108
S. THOMAS'S, KUCHING. Mr. Gregg	110
FAMILY OF CHRISTIAN DYAKS. Dr. C. Hose	114
BISHOP CHAMBERS	118
BISHOP HOSE. Photo., Elliot & Fry	118
BANTING DYAKS. Mr. Gregg	120
LUJAI, UKIT OF THE UPPER REJANG. Dr. C. Hose	122

LIST OF ILLUSTRATIONS

	TO FACE PAGE
Kayan Girl	126
Boys at Merdang School	126
Christ Church, Banting. Mr. Gregg	128
Christ Church, Lundu. Mr. Gregg	132
S. Michael's, Sandakan. Mr. Gregg	134
S. John's, Merdang, Interior	138
Gathering Pepper	146
Mengatal. British North Borneo Co.	146
Skerang Women. By permission of Miss Bunyon	150
S. Thomas's Boys' School, Kuching. Mr. Gregg	154
Aben Deng, a Longwat Chief. Dr. C. Hose	156
Tribal Map. Mr. Ling Roth	

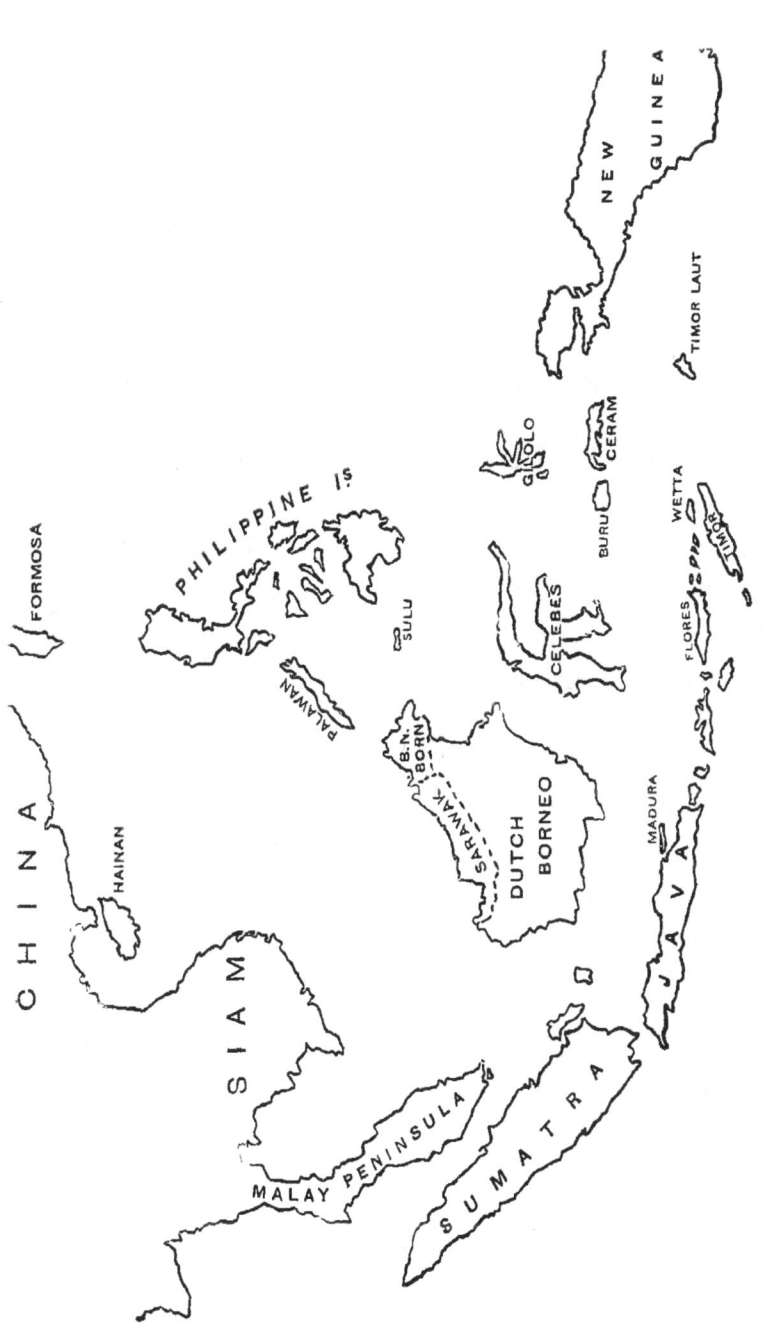

Sketch Map to show General Surroundings of Borneo.

CHAPTER I

Borneo and its Riches

ONE of the uttermost parts of the earth, 8,000 miles from England, a country as large as Germany and Poland together! Leaving Australia, as a continent, out of count, New Guinea, the home of the frizzy-headed Papuan, is the only island in the world of greater extent than BORNEO — this land of river and of palm, where dwells the sad-faced, smooth-haired Dyak.

To reach it you travel down the Channel, across the Bay of Biscay, through the Straits of Gibraltar, the whole length of the Mediterranean, the Suez Canal and the Red Sea, down the Indian Ocean to Ceylon, then across the Bay of Bengal and through the Malacca Straits to Singapore. There you would leave the large ocean liner, and tranship into a smaller vessel in which to cross the 417 miles of the South China Sea to Sarawak in Borneo.

The island covers now an area of some 900 by 700 miles. Long ago it was not so large, but many small islands fringed its coasts. As centuries rolled on the large rivers brought down to their mouths extensive alluvial deposits which spread to the outlying islands, and so many of them became incorporated with the mainland. In the Landak territory this extension of land has been so great that almost all the ground west of the Kandang Mountains has been formed in this way in the last four centuries. The coast of Borneo, especially on the west, is therefore much less irregular than that of most of the neighbouring countries. There are many rivers, which are of great importance as the only means of communication, but some have large sandbanks at the mouth and some have bores, or tidal waves, sometimes twelve feet high, so that they cannot be navigated by large vessels.

The map of Borneo shows that two-thirds of the country, that lying on the east and south, is under the rule of the Dutch, who have large industries, and carry on an important trade with other countries. With the Dutch part, however, we are not dealing in this book, but only with the remaining third, yet large enough, for it is nearly the size of the United Kingdom.

The westernmost point of the island is Cape Datu, and here the territory of the Rajah of Sarawak begins. The position of the stars in the constellation of Cassiopeia gives an idea of the coast-line as it trends northwards, jutting out at Cape Sirik and

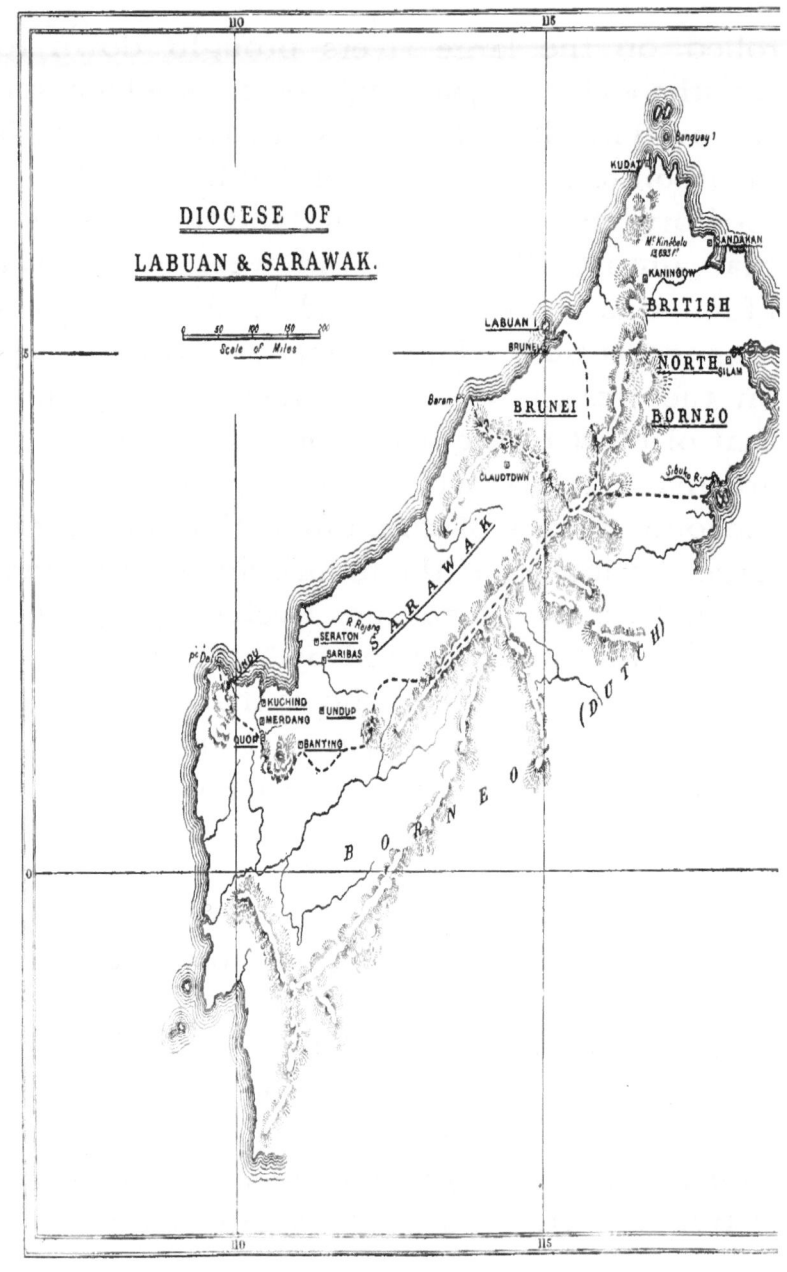

again at Baram Point; the narrow strip of Sarawak is interrupted here, and there comes then a small wedge of country called Brunei, still nominally governed by its own Sultan. Beyond this the two rivers Limbang and Lawas belong to Sarawak, then the northern part of the island right across, like the apex of a pyramid, is under the rule of the British North Borneo Company, and is worked by them for exports of coal, manganese, tobacco, camphor, rubber and other commodities. This part alone is larger than Ireland. Thirty miles off the coast of this northern part lies Labuan, an island ten miles long by five miles broad, a Crown Colony, administered by the Governor of the Straits Settlements. Though so small in extent, it is important from its position, its good harbour, its valuable fields of coal, and from being a station of the Eastern Extension Cable Company; from it, too, the Diocese of Labuan takes its name.

The chief towns on the mainland are Kuching, the capital of Sarawak, with a population of about 15,000; Brunei, the city of the Sultan, which has been satirically called the Venice of the East, with 10,000 people; and Sandakan and Jesselton in British North Borneo.

As you approach Borneo you would find the sea very shallow, and you would look with delight towards the land which seems covered with fresh, green vegetation, and here and there are thickly wooded hills with a mountain range behind. This chief range runs from Cape Datu to the north-east; it forms the watershed and ends at its highest point in Mount Kini-balu in the north, 13,500 feet high. The rocks are limestone, slate, sandstone, conglomerate, and the highest points are of crystalline schist and granite. To-day there are no volcanoes, but old craters give evidence that these did exist ages ago. Some of the higher peaks are sharply conical and needle-shaped, like the formation of the Dolomites.

Many rivers rise in this chain: on the east the Sibuco, the Koti, the Sambas and Kipuas, the Kalabacking, the Sugut; on the west the Brunei, the Baram, Bintulu, Rejang, Krian, Sarebas, Batang-Lupar, Sadong and Sarawak. The Rejang is navigable for 120 miles of its course; its delta covers 1,600 square miles and has a coast-line of 60 miles. The many rivers broaden in places into many lagoons, but there are no lakes.

The climate of Borneo in the lower country is damp and hot, trying to Europeans, but it is certainly not unhealthy; and on the higher ground it is much drier. The length of the day never varies, for the island lies just on the Equator, so the sun rises about 6 A.M. and sets about 6 P.M. all the year round with hardly any twilight. Nearly every day brings some rain, but even in the rainy season, from November to March, there is seldom a wholly wet day, though during those months there are often violent storms of rain with wind and thunder. The average temperature has no extremes, ranging from 74° to 93° Fahrenheit.

As you made closer acquaintance with the green vegetation which you saw on the coast you would find it to be chiefly coarse jungle grass, useless and unhealthy, but behind and among this rank grass are growing trees of wonderful beauty. If you were bound for Kuching you would enter the country by going up the Sarawak River. In a direct line Kuching is only five miles from the coast, but the river winds fully five times as much, so that you would travel twenty-five miles. What would you see as you made this journey? First, close down to the water's edge, the graceful mangroves, lit up at night by myriads of fireflies flitting about like wandering stars in the darkness, then the short nipa-palm, with its leaves bending gently down, leaves used when dried to make the mat walls and the roofs of houses. Farther back grow the tall nibong-palms whose straight, strong stems form the posts of native dwellings and the piles on which they are raised. And in the forests farther back?

There is the *bilian*, the iron-wood, which must be

used in building if churches, schools and houses are not to be "eaten down" by white ants. Then there is the mohor tree, eighty feet high, with timber strong and springy for boat-building, and the kaladang tree, reaching a height of a hundred feet, straight and tough for masts; of these woods, cargoes have been sent to our English dockyards. Ebony, too, grows here.

The cocoa-nut is one of the many palms, the betel-nut another. This has a tall, slender stem with a bunch of yellow-husked nuts hanging under its crown of leaves. Betel-chewing is one of the Malay fashions which is followed by the Dyaks and by many of the Chinese. They spread lime (got from burnt shells) on the leaf of a pepper vine called *sirih*, wrap it up with tobacco, with some of the scraped betel-nut and a little gambier, and chew it as a narcotic. An ornamental betel box or bag is carried about as one of their toilet accessories. The juice is bright red so their lips become stained that colour, and the teeth are stained an ugly dark brown. The effect of chewing is to produce giddiness at first, to burn the mouth and to deaden the sense of taste. Yet for all this the "fashion" has lasted for over two thousand years.

Another palm provides us with sago, and half the sago in the world comes from the palms grown on the banks of the Oya Mukah and other rivers in

Cocoanut Grove.

Borneo. The pith is the part used, and to obtain it the tree has to be cut down; the stem is then sawn into lengths, split open and the pith grated to a coarse powder; this is washed in many waters, the starchy deposit is allowed to settle and is forced through sieves, whence it drops as the round grains of pearl sago.

Yet another palm, a climbing one, is the rattan. We shall see that it is used by the Dyaks for bracelets and waist rings, but it is exported, too, in great quantities to make the cane seats for chairs and sofas.

Camphor is one of the most valuable exports. That from Borneo is known as hard camphor, and is bought by the Chinese for as much as fifty times the price of ordinary camphor. It is obtained by cutting down the tree and splitting it into small pieces, when the camphor is found in clear crystal blocks, hidden in hollows in the wood.

Sixty years ago an Indian doctor noticed that the Malays made curious handles to their knives; he discovered that they used the milky juice found between the wood and the bark of a tree, which dried into a solid and rather elastic mass. He introduced it into England for various uses in surgery, and for coating submarine telegraph wires. This is the gutta-percha of Borneo, but it is less used than formerly.

Rubber is one of the most valuable products in the world. Like gutta it consists of a sap, found in many plants, *e.g.*, in the stem of a climber named Willoughbsia; the creamy liquid is collected, and, by the addition of nipa salt, congealed into rough balls.

But towering as a king above all the forest is the tapang tree, rising in one single stem often 100 feet high, before it branches under its dome of beautiful foliage. It spreads out so widely above the roots that from its buttresses planks large enough to make a billiard table can be cut, in colour like dark oak, and polishing well.

There are, besides, the bamboo, the sugar-cane, and many fruit trees: the bushowa, like an Orleans plum, with the taste of a mango; the durian, bearing a fruit the size of a man's head, covered outside with spikes like a hedgehog; the ten or twelve seeds are as large as pigeon's eggs, and the pulp round them is creamy and delicious, though its *scent* suggests a mixture of rotten eggs, sugar and onions. The mangosteen, *the* fruit of the East, is of a deep, rich red colour, and clear inside like an opal.

These are the names of only a few of the trees which form the marvellous forest vegetation.

As you go through the forests you *may* meet an elephant or a rhinoceros; you *will* meet monkeys, the orang-outan, found only here and in Sumatra,

Sapong Rubber Estate.

as well as others; you may see wild boars, honey-bears, buffalo and deer, and squirrels will leap over your head. Darting among the trees you will see gorgeous butterflies, birds of wondrous plumage, parrots, pigeons, the sun bird, the argus, the bulwer, with an eagle or a vulture soaring up above, and if you are with Dyaks you will perforce *hear* as well as see, for their intense listening for the voice of certain birds will make you listen too, though in your superior knowledge you scoff at the omens which keep your poor ignorant brother in bondage. When you need a rest you will see to it that you do not mistake a coiled-up snake for the inviting roots of a tree, and when, hot and dusty, you want to bathe in a river you will look out for the crocodiles which abound.

Then beneath the earth what store of wealth! Coal in extensive workings both in Labuan and in Sarawak; gold, diamonds, quicksilver, tin, iron of such quality, and smelted and worked so well, that the weapons made excel those of Europe in strength and fineness of edge. Antimony, a metal which neither tarnishes nor rusts, and is therefore of great value for printers' type and other articles. Much of the ore from which it is smelted used to be brought to England from Borneo.

Tortoiseshell, from the many turtles found on the shores, and beeswax, are two other valuable products. The bees make their homes on the top of the tapang tree, so high that they can see, as in a field below them, where the best flowers are; from these they cull the sweetness, and make, it is said, the best honey in the world and a great quantity of wax. Smoke from fires lit at the foot of the tree drives the bees away and then the Dyak boys climb up and take the wax and honey.

Out of the many other objects of commerce only three more can be mentioned, three bought by the Chinese alone. Birds'-nests, the edible nests of a swallow, are one of their greatest dainties; the best are transparent like woven isinglass, and are made into soup supposed to be specially strengthening and very delicious. They are found in the caves which honeycomb the limestone rocks in many parts of Borneo, and are taken three or four times a year by the natives who form nesting parties and reap in their gains. In Sarawak the profits are divided between the Government and the tribe in whose territory the caves are. The results of the first and third nest hunts go to the men who gather in the nests, those of the middle "take" to the Government. The birds are like the ordinary swallow in colour but about half as large. Some of the caves are of enormous extent, rising up into vaulted domes, which, as well as the sides, are covered by thousands of the nests firmly glued to

RAPID ON THE PARAN RIVER.
(Rejang District.)

MAIAS.
(In the Sarawak Museum.)

the rock. Old nests are dark and mixed with feathers, so care is taken to seek out the clear, pale yellow ones. Frail-looking ladders and scaffoldings of rattan are put up inside the caves, and from these the Dyaks reach the nests by means of long poles, bearing at the end two prongs above a lighted candle; this enables them to see the nest in the darkness of the cave; one man having detached it from its foundation, it is taken off the prongs by another, standing below. In some cases the caves are in the face of the cliff and can only be reached by boys let down by ropes from the top.

The second object of desire of the Chinese we should like even less—*trepang*—a sea-slug, sold also for making soup. The third is *blachan*, a sort of caviare, made of shrimps and small fish, dried in the sun and pounded.

Few countries contribute so much as this far-off island to the wealth and comfort of European nations.

Think of it! The coal you burn perhaps abroad, the type of the newspaper you read, the gold in the ring you wear, the quicksilver in your thermometer, the cane of the chair you sit upon, the wax which polishes your floor, the camphor which preserves your furs, the sago and rice for your puddings, the pepper in your soup, the india-rubber of your galoshes, to say nothing of your coffee and tobacco, all this you may owe to the one island of Borneo.

You pay for them? Yes, but we are learning now, at last, that our conscience must go beyond the mere money exchange, and that we must ask how and by whom the things we use are made. We have a responsibility which current coin cannot discharge, a responsibility for *human lives and souls*.

The voice of the forest swayed by the breeze, the fragrance of flower and leaf borne up as incense on high, the fruit and the bud yielding its life to satisfy ours, bring us a vision of purpose fulfilled. God made them for use, for glory and for beauty, and surely in a land of growth so luxuriant He looks down and sees Nature fulfilling His will. " O let the earth bless the Lord, yea, let it praise Him and magnify Him for ever."

When we have sung of the sun and the moon, of the snow and the ice, of the seas and the floods, of all the powers of the universe praising the Lord; of the fishes, of the birds, of the beasts, then we call on the children of men. Do *they* praise Him? We have risen through the scale of creation to that which should be the highest praise. Where is this note which the Lord of all is listening for? Does He hear *that* from the forests of Borneo?

Who, then, are the children of men there for whose praise the Father waits? Let us see the many races.

I. *The Malays*, the old ruling class and the aristocracy of Borneo. They belong to the Mongolian family which came originally from the highlands of Asia. Those who settled in Sumatra and in Java, whence they crossed to Borneo, belong to the Indo-Malay branch. For centuries they governed the island under the various Sultans, but this government consisted chiefly in extorting as much as possible from the people, and when Rajah Brooke took over Sarawak he found the natives were being mulcted on barter sometimes to the extent of no less than 2,000 per cent. An unregulated system of oppression and forced contributions, farmed out from the Sultans downwards, had resulted in a network of cruelty and corruption; we shall see that under enlightened rule these people have learnt much and are now trusted members of the Rajah's council.

The Malays are not a tall people, averaging but little over five feet in height, light brown in colour, with well-shaped heads, straight eyes, large and dark, rather flat noses and high cheek bones; their wrists and ankles are small and well formed; most of them have straight black hair, but there are a considerable number in whom Caucasian blood can be traced. These are taller and stronger, a lighter brown in colour, with brown wavy hair and symmetrical figures. All the Malays are Mohammedans, and their example influences the natives.

Here is one of the great calls to us, if we believe that to us has been entrusted a higher faith to offer to the natives.

II. *The Chinese.*—The traders, farmers, and miners working with infinite patience in washing out gold and securing antimony. Besides these Chinese immigrants there are also the descendants of many Chinese who in past ages intermarried with Dyak women, and who form a large Dyak-Chinese population. In Borneo, as in many other countries to which the Chinaman goes, the one aim for which he toils is that he may be able to return to end his days, and to be buried in his native land, to earn money, honestly and by patient industry, but to earn and to save enough to keep him " at home," where he probably has a Chinese wife, as well as his Dyak wife in Borneo. For this reason the conversion of the Chinese is of the utmost importance. Our opportunity is here, to help towards what has been said to be the only means by which the " Yellow Peril " may be averted, a " religious triumph," a " miraculous spread of Christianity in its best form ". Every Chinaman to whom is brought the knowledge of Christ's love may become a centre of evangelisation to his own countrymen, not only in Borneo, but when he goes back to his fatherland. The constancy of the Chinese in the Boxer persecution has shown us that they are worth winning, and here we have the opportunity of many ready to hear. In Borneo, as elsewhere, the Chinese are awakening to the value of Western education. They will get knowledge, and if we fail, they will get mere learning alone without the knowledge of God.

III. *The Tamils.*—Many Indians, chiefly from the Madras Presidency, have gone to Borneo to work as navvies and coolies. The slim figures and bright clothes of these so-called Klings, both men and women, make a picturesque sight as they work on the roads, the tiny children following close to their mothers. The police, too, are Indians, but these belong to the fine race of Sikhs.

IV. *The Dyaks.*—These aborigines are by far the most numerous, as well as the most interesting of the 600,000 people in the Diocese of Labuan and Sarawak. The name is used here (for convenience of division), as it is often, but wrongly, used, to denote all the native inhabitants, not Malay. Nearly one hundred and fifty different tribes have, however, been classified, to only fifty of whom the name Dyak is properly applied. The word is thought to be derived from *daya*, the generic term for *man* in the Land-Dyak language, which thus came into use as the designation of certain tribes. There are two chief branches of the Dyaks, the Land- and Sea-Dyaks. Probably the Land-Dyaks came first from the mainland, and, later, were driven back into the highlands by the more vigorous race of Sea-Dyaks who followed them from the same part.

The Land-Dyaks.—These occupy the south-west corner of Sarawak, inland from the fringe of Malay population which inhabits the coast. They are slightly built, rather taller, and rather redder in colour than the Malays, and with better features, though the flat-bridged nose, the wide nostrils and large mouth common to all Dyaks do not form a type of beauty in European eyes. Their hair is black and straight; hardly any have beards or whiskers, except in one village, where men with goat-like beards were met with. The lands of different tribes are generally bounded by rivers, and the villages are built not far from the banks; on the head-waters the people are usually peaceable agriculturists, but nearer the coast they used often to join the Malays in their sea-raids.

Just below the beautiful Santubong Mountain, at the mouth of the Sarawak River, curious gold ornaments and earthenware have been dug up which may be relics of a far-back colony of Peguans from Rangoon.

The Sea-Dyaks have the country north and east of the Land-Dyaks; they were pressed inland by the Malay invasion, but have always kept close to the rivers. Active life as pirates and seafarers has developed them into a stronger and more vigorous race, more broadly built, yet with light and graceful carriage. In colour they are yellower than the Land-Dyaks, but their hair is just as black and long.

North of these Sea-Dyaks, up to the border of the Sultanate of Brunei, come the Kayans and Kenniahs. They are said to number 10,000, and they stretch right across into Dutch territory; they are lighter in colour, stouter in build than the Dyaks, and their language is quite different. One tribe among them, the Punans, is thought by some writers to be the purest type of aborigines; they are strong and large-boned, and have better manners than any of the other peoples. They neither build houses nor plant paddy, and are the one tribe which has never practised head-hunting. The Ukits are probably allied to the Punans; they live in the hill country (whence their name, from Bukit, *hill* in Malay); they are tall and slim, with refined features and beautiful hands.

The Bisayans, handsome, fair and light-hearted, who go over to Labuan to work the coal, and then gamble away their wages, and the Milanaus, whose girls are as fair as any Europeans and the belles of Borneo, are only two more among the many peoples in Sarawak.

Passing on to North Borneo the tribes are fewer in number, and generally of a lower type.

The Bajaus, or Sea Gypsies, a race with low foreheads and pinched faces, come, tradition says, from Johore, where they lived always in boats; on one of their festivals all the boats were fastened astern of their prince's vessel, when a storm came and blew them all across to Borneo. In memory of this they keep the anniversary by a general bathing, and they still live in small covered boats, or in houses built out into the sea on piles.

The Muruts are in great numbers in North Borneo; they are the lowest type of native, coarse, dirty and ugly. In height, language and customs they are entirely different from the Dyaks, but where they have been brought into contact with civilisation and kindly treated they have shown themselves friendly and hospitable.

The Dusuns people great part of the interior of British North Borneo; near the coast they wear more clothing than most tribes, but the farther inland the fewer clothes, till at last all they wear is made from the bark of trees.

The Lanuns, supposed to have come from the Philippines, are Mohammedans and are dying out; they were one of the most aggressive tribes in their wild piracy, raiding not only the coasts, but stealing away the children of the Dusuns and Ida'an.

Peoples, beneath their wildness, docile, earnest, affectionate and very responsive to kindness, such

Kayans Collecting Gutta Percha.

are these children of the jungle, who appeal with attractive power to European hearts.

There are still vast tracts of land along the hills of Sarawak and in the interior of North Borneo unexplored, but English enterprise will some day develop the country, and doubtless these new regions will yield wealth equal to the old, yet those riches of commerce are not the greatest; the glory of the island waits for the greater riches of human life. What that life becomes depends on us.

" That our garners may be full and plenteous with all manner of store." Yes! all manner of store; it seems as though scarce any were lacking to contribute to the rich abundance. " That there be no leading into captivity and no complaining in our streets. Blessed are the people who are in such a case." The days of captivity and of slavery are over. The tribes, no longer hunted from place to place, can be approached in settled villages; freed from the constant outlook of defence, they have leisure for peaceful occupations; looking up to the white man who has brought them this security they wonder dumbly, has he no more to bring? They are blessed so far, but " Yea, blessed are the people who have the LORD FOR THEIR GOD ".

Six thousand Christians out of a population of 600,000—one in every 100! Of these many are falling back for lack of shepherding.

The condition of many Christians is heart-rending, and it is all due to the neglect of the Church which has left them without missionaries—in some places for years and years. When shall the fulness of the Gentiles be brought in, and the praise of inanimate creation be crowned by the praise of the children of men?

QUESTIONS ON CHAPTER I

1. What do you know of Labuan, its position, size and government; has it an importance out of proportion to its size, and why?

2. Are there any large towns in Borneo?

3. What do you know about the rivers, the trees, the wild animals?

4. What sort of climate has Borneo?

5. What articles in common use, domestic or otherwise, are found there, and are there any minerals?

6. In what way is China commercially interested in Borneo?

7. What are the different races of inhabitants?

8. How many tribes may be roughly included in the general term "Dyak"?

9. Has civilisation introduced any, and, if so, all the possible, blessings?

10. We pay our debts, in current coin, for the imports we receive; does that discharge our responsibility?

11. Why should we be especially anxious that the Chinese in Borneo should become Christian?

CHAPTER II

The People and their Customs

THE habits and manners of life of peoples so different in race, and of tribes, some living on the sea-board and up the rivers, others in the hills or among the jungle, present necessarily great diversity.

The Malays have the heritage of ruling blood and the present position of importance as giving members to the Rajah's Council. Some of them are wealthy and live luxuriously. Their national dress is rather magnificent: a turban edged with transparent gold lace or fringe, loose trousers of striped cotton or silk, and a white cotton or silk jacket. Round the waist they wear a *sarong*, a long scarf, through which is hung the *kris*, their war-knife. The women wear bright-coloured clothes, sometimes of satin, and sarongs inwoven with gold thread, jackets covered with gold ornaments and fastened with gold brooches. Of course as Mohammedans they have strict rules as to their hours of prayer and as to food, and some of them go on pilgrimage to Mecca, but they are not as a rule very particular about their religion except, perhaps, in regard to certain forms, and they are very ignorant. When Sir James Brooke undertook the government of Sarawak he promised to respect the religion of the country, therefore no mission work has been done among the Malays in Sarawak, nor, handicapped as the Church has been by the smallness of staff, has it been possible to attempt anything in Brunei, a purely native state untouched by Western rule. Through years of misrule and lawlessness the Malay character deteriorated, and the lower classes are said to be untrustworthy and dangerous, but they are apt to learn, and it is ours to set before them the vision of truth and righteousness.

In every undeveloped country the Chinese seem better adapted than any other race to bring out the wealth of nature, possessing just those qualities of diligence, ability and willingness to endure hardship which are needed. In some parts of Borneo, where they are employed in large numbers in mines, they form communities of their own, and keep their native customs. In Kuching most of the shops are kept by Chinamen; they have no glass windows, so the wares are open to the passers-by in the daytime, but at night they are shuttered. There are several joss-houses there; one old one is especially

Exterior of Sea-Dyak Long House.

(By W. T. Hornaday—"Two Years in the Jungle".)

THE PEOPLE AND THEIR CUSTOMS   23

picturesque, its wide portico lit up by red-coloured lanterns which at night throw a rosy light on the trees around.

But we must leave these incomers and pass on to see the life of the aboriginal inhabitants.

There are a few tribes who have not attained to the art of building even the rudest dwellings, but crouch round the trunks of trees. By far the greater number of natives, however, live in the "long houses," of which the Land- and Sea-Dyaks' dwellings are examples. They are always raised on posts, four, eight, twelve or even twenty feet high, and so, in mid-air, in one building 400 or 500 feet long, is housed a population of perhaps 500 people. The largest house written of is 771 feet long. The following description is based upon one given by Mr. Brooke Low from observations of Mr. Crosland.

"A Sea-Dyak village is a terrace upon posts, varying in length according to the number of houses of which it is composed, and as the various houses are built according to a single scale and measurement and by a combination of labour, they rarely fail to present a uniform and regular appearance.

"There is always a ladder at either end of the terrace by which to ascend, and sometimes one or more towards the centre of the *tanju* or open-air platform. The roof is thatched throughout with the same material—shingles or palm leaves ; if the latter the *nipa* leaves are used when procurable. The flooring in some villages is made of stems of palm-trees split into laths, and in other cases of cane, bamboo or even twigs. The laths or bamboos allow a delicious current of air to permeate the apartment. The outer walls are of plank or nipa leaves, the inner of bark. No nails are used, the beams or rafters are lashed together with rattan and secured by wooden pegs. The posts are innumerable and of hard wood. The village in time of war is surrounded at its base by a wooden palisade, which is itself protected by chevaux-de-frise of pointed bamboo. The village is divided by plank walling into two main portions, the front and the rear. The former partakes of the nature of a very wide verandah and is open throughout its entire length. The latter occupies the rear of the entire building and is subdivided into apartments, one for each family. Between the plank wall and the edge of the *ruai* is the *tempuan* or footway, a narrow passage running through the centre, so that a person may walk from one end of the village to the other without encountering many obstacles.

"Every family thus possesses a compact little residence to itself, comprising a *bilik* or room where they can enjoy privacy when they like, a *tempuan* or thoroughfare where they pound their rice and pile

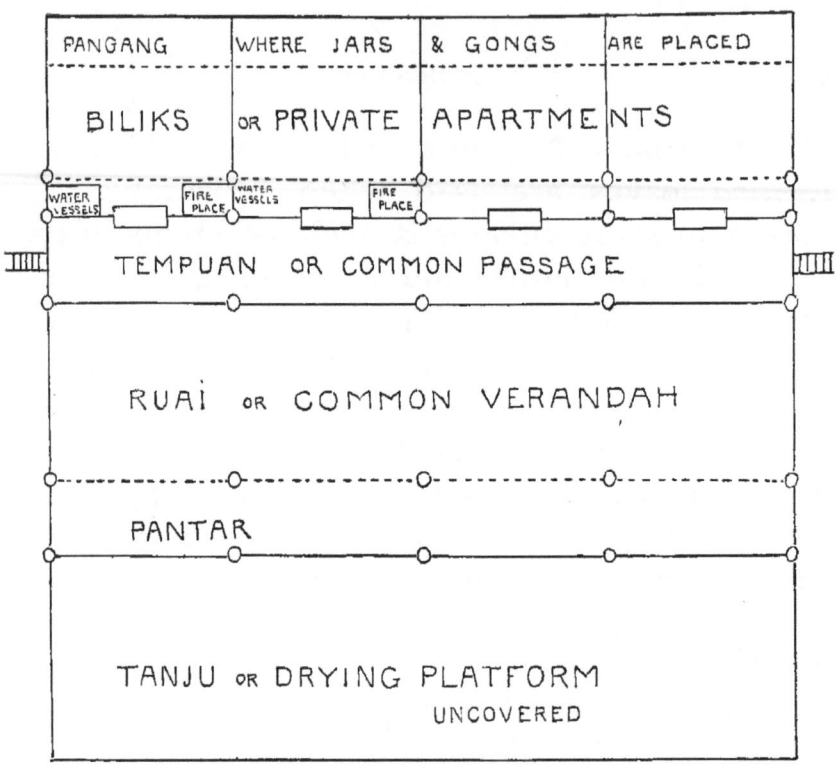

DIAGRAMMATIC PLAN OF SEA-DYAK HOUSE.
F. W. Leggatt.

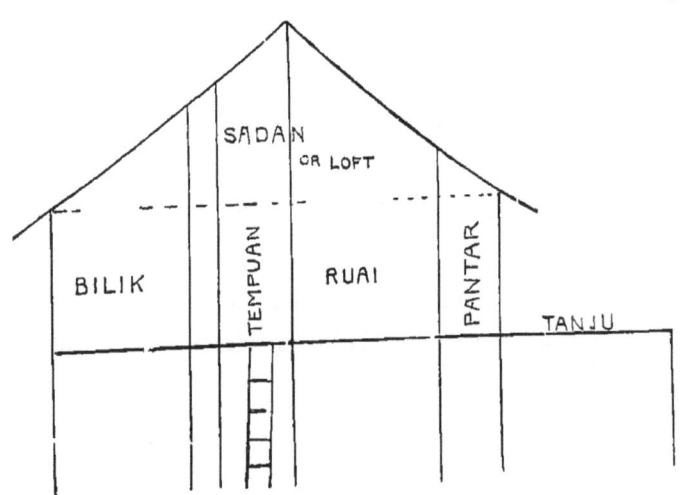

DIAGRAM OF SECTION OF SEA-DYAK HOUSE.
From a Sketch by Mr. Crosland.

up their firewood, a *ruai* or verandah where they receive visitors, a *tanju* or open-air platform where they dry their grain, air their things and lounge in the cool of the evening, and a *sadau* or loft where they keep their tools and store their paddy.

"The *bilik* or private apartment is furnished with a swinging door which opens outwards, and is closed by means of a heavy weight suspended by a thong to the inside. The door can be secured when required by means of a bar . . . There is no window such as we understand, but a portion of the roof is so constructed that it can be raised a foot or two by means of a stick to let out the smoke, or to admit the fresh air. If the neighbours are relations or intimate friends, as is often the case, a hole is cut in the wall which separates the rooms to avoid the necessity of a roundabout way into each other's apartments, and some villages are so arranged that one can traverse the entire length of the rear section of the building by means of these apartments without appearing on the verandah at all. There is no furniture in the room, none in fact being required. The floor is the occupier's table, and they squat to their meals. But there are plenty of mats to sit upon, and baskets to pack their clothes in. Their cups and plates are hung in rows upon the walls as much for ornament as for use. Their valuables, such as old jars, gongs, etc., are ranged on three sides, so as to present the most imposing appearance of wealth. But the room is stuffy and untidy, and no wonder seeing that there is but one for each family, and this one is used as a kitchen as well as a messroom, as a nursery as well as a bedchamber. There can be no absolute privacy unless the door is barred to exclude the neighbours. Boys and girls keep running in and out, and the dogs are always on the watch in the *tempuan* to spring in whenever the door swings open. The floor is swept after a fashion, but the room is never dusted, and the roof is simply black with soot. In the more lofty houses the refuse is thrown into the piggery and poultry-yard, which occupies the area or waste place under the house, and the stench in most cases is better imagined than described. The *dapur* or fireplace is the only real piece of furniture in the room. It is built either to the right or to the left of the door, set up against the wall of the *tempuan* and resembles an open cupboard, the lowest shelf resting upon the floor, and the upper shelves being of lattice-work instead of plank. The former is boarded all round and filled with clay. This is the fireplace, and it is furnished with a few stones between which the pots are set. The shelf immediately above the fire is set apart for smoking fish, meat, etc. The shelves above this again are filled with firewood which, being thoroughly dried, is ready

THE PEOPLE AND THEIR CUSTOMS 27

for use. The women, who do the cooking, have also to keep these shelves supplied from the pile in the *tempuan*. As the smoke from the wood fire is not conducted to the roof by means of a chimney it spreads itself through the loft, and blackens the beams and rafters until it finds its way out by the open window.

"The *tempuan* or general thoroughfare is between the *bilik* and the *ruai*. It is three feet in width and is paved with wood. . . . The *ruai* or verandah is in front of the *tempuan* and is as nearly as possible the same size as the *bilik*, from which it differs principally in being open on all sides and without any partition. It is therefore a cooler and more agreeable place, and as such is frequented by both sexes for the purposes of conversation, discussion and indoor pursuits. Female visitors are usually received in the *bilik*, but male visitors are invariably received in the *ruai* and only enter the *bilik* when invited to do so to be introduced to the women and to share the meals. They sleep in the *ruai* along with the boys and bachelors, and sit there all day when they have nothing better to do, conversing with the head of the family and chewing betel. . . . Some *ruais* are provided with a panggan or bedstead, with plank sides, in one corner of the space for the men to sleep in, but this is not always the case. If the head of the family has made it for his own use, and if he be a chief or rich man, he will fix his gongs of various kinds around it for the sake of show; his weapons will be within reach, and his war-dress will hang from the roof where it can be seen to the best advantage—a skull cap of wicker-work with its nodding plumes, and a skin jacket decorated with the tail feathers of the war-bird of his tribe. But by far the most valuable ornament in the *ruai* is of course the bunch of human heads which hangs over the fireplace like a bunch of fruits: these are the heads obtained on various war-paths by various members of the family, dead and living, and are handed down from father to son as the most precious heirlooms, more precious even than the ancient jars which they prize so highly.

"The *tanju* or open-air platform is in front of the *ruai* and is railed at the edge, but the rail is often so slight that it is unsafe to lean against it. The flooring is occasionally of ironwood to stand exposure to the weather. It is used as a lounge in the evening, the view from it being [sometimes] extensive and the breeze refreshing. While the sun is shining the paddy is put out to dry, as are the clothes and a variety of other things. The family whetstone and dye vat are kept here under the eaves of the roof."

The ladder leading up to the house is generally

the trunk of a tree in which notches are cut for steps, and the same kind of ladder leads from the *ruai* to the *sadau* or loft above, in which the paddy, the agricultural implements and seed are stored away.

When the nipa palm is used for the roofs or partitions it is made into *atap* very cleverly arranged. The fronds of the palm have leaves from two to six feet long and three inches broad growing out of each side of the centre rib: these leaves are doubled over a stick, one row overlapping each other from right to left, the next from left to right, and they are then sewn down with rattan; in this way a kind of leaf-tile is formed impervious to rain and sun. When bamboo is used for the floors a long stem is split open, soaked in water and beaten out flat: this makes slabs eight to eighteen inches wide, and when stained by the tread and soot of years the floor might be taken for old and polished oak or walnut. Of tapang wood, black and polished too by use, are the seats of the chiefs, the only furniture which is valued and handed down for generations.

When these Sea-Dyaks want to migrate the inhabitants of the house are called to meet in council. The men sit in a circle on their mats, chewing betel and smoking, the women and children sit behind: the discussion is long, and it is often no easy matter for the chief to keep the peace. Dissentients may split off and join another " house," but if the move is decided on some of the oldest men are sent to search out the land : when they have chosen a place the birds must be consulted. The cry of a bird must be heard which foretells health and good fortune ; then a piece of wood is hung up on the spot, and this *Kaya burong* guards the ground. If the omens are favourable the land is cleared and marked out ; the jungle must be cut not burnt, for to a burnt clearing plagues and sicknesses will come. Then a bamboo is set up and filled with water, a spear and shield beside it warn off meddlers, and a rail protects it from animals. This is a practical way of testing the healthiness of the spot by the amount of evaporation, but besides people and wild beasts, the spirits must be kept from interfering, so watchers beat the tom-toms all night to prevent their coming.

If the water decrease much it forebodes continued famine, but if the result is satisfactory then the house may be begun. Each family must kill a pig or a fowl so that propitiatory blood may be sprinkled on the posts, or in some cases the post is driven into the ground through the live fowl. These posts, of which there are a great number, are from eight to eighteen inches in diameter, and, as we saw, from four to twenty feet high, and they must be of bilian or other hard wood : a hole four feet deep is made for each post, which is tilted into it by means of a roller. The Milanaus used always to have their houses raised forty feet for safety, but under the Rajah's rule Sarawak is now too peaceable to need such precautions. In a Sea-Dyak village where two Englishmen were murdered in 1857 the posts of the houses were also forty feet high, for the people said they were often attacked by the Kayans, who would draw one of their large war-boats on land; this they turned over, and the men getting under it carried it on their heads as a shield. They crashed through the frail palisades round the house, and getting beneath it hacked away at the posts under cover of their boat shield; the large hard posts were so strong that the dwellers above could sometimes drive off the enemy by letting down stones and beams to break through the boat, but the besiegers on *terra firma* held the vantage ground, and axe and fire generally won the day by the downfall of the house.

The Kenniah houses are much smaller, generally three in a row, and the Dusuns make a second storey in which they take refuge when the lower floor is under water.

The Land-Dyaks make many paths—straight up over the hills, through the jungle and across the rivers—paths which bring the unwary European to sudden falls. They are made of the stems of trees, generally three inches in diameter; the rough bark is cut off on the upper side, and a succession of single stems is laid on supports two feet, or even six feet above the ground. Sir Charles Brooke describes the paths as "An introduction to a new style of walking resembling tight-rope manœuvring more than any other". Sometimes instead of trees bamboos are laid side by side; these paths are called *batangs*. The bridges are more picturesque than safe. A bamboo is slung from branches of a tree on one side of the river to those on the other, or if one bamboo is not long enough, two are tied together with rattan, others fastened from higher branches are crossed below them as supports, and to these a hand-rail is fastened; this exalted bridge is reached from the banks by sloping ladders made, like those leading to the houses, of notched tree trunks. In some places a single tree trunk, given to turning round, is laid from bank to bank across a river, and in others wood and bamboo are so cleverly fastened together as to form a suspension bridge 50 or 60 feet high across a river 100 feet in width.

These paths lead to Land-Dyak villages planted in lovely spots, often on a hill-side for protection, so that the houses being more difficult of access, there is no need for the massed population, and the houses are much smaller; near some stream too,

Traveller's Palm.

Dyak Bridge.

whence water is brought close to the houses in bamboo aqueducts, carried like the *batangs* on high supports.

Each tribe has its own chief, but the method of election varies. Among these Land-Dyaks, the Orang Kaya is chosen by the votes of the married men. Each of the "houses" has its *tuah* or elder who is responsible for its order; his room is in the centre; near him are the richer people who are able to entertain visitors, and at the ends of the house are placed the bravest to defend it. All the tuahs form the Orang Kaya's council; they try and punish offenders, and for tribal matters have a Home Rule, independent of the Rajah's overlordship, but the Orang Kaya's tenure of authority depends on his own personal influence. Many Orang Kayas are recognised by the Rajah and confirmed in their office by his appointment.

Personal fashions are applied chiefly to the hair, teeth and ears. A pair of tweezers is an indispensable toilet article, and with these every hair is plucked out from the faces of both men and women, even to the eyebrows and eyelashes. Teeth are always stained black by coating them with a resinous liquid obtained by heating cocoa-nut or other woods; they are filed into various shapes, sometimes into sharp points, or even almost level with the gum, sometimes like a saw, or again into a succession of concavities; often they are drilled with holes into which an ornament of brass wire is fitted as a stud, but with all this manipulation the people hardly know what toothache is. Possibly the black gum, or the areca nut which they chew, preserves their teeth.

Except that in many tribes the lobes of the ears are slit and most horribly dragged down, the only actual deformity in vogue seems to be that of flattening the foreheads of the children by a board strapped on, which is practised by the Milanaus.

Dress ranges up a long gamut from the undressed *tatu* of the Kayans to the sumptuous materials and brilliant colouring affected by the Malays. The Dyaks tatu a little, but the Kayan women are covered on their arms, the back of their hands, and from the waist to below the knee; the designs are often very good, and so fine that at a distance the effect is that of dark clothing. Among the Kayan men the amount of tatu represents their record of courage. For bravery in battle or for head-taking, the backs of the hands are done, but if the owner has only been present at a fight and has not killed a person for himself, only one of his fingers may be adorned. Some tribes tatu the appearance of the beards and whiskers which they lack.

The Punans tatu their faces as well as the body

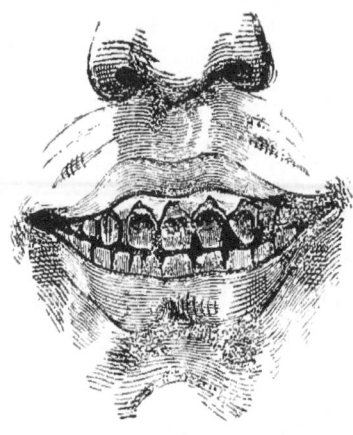

Dyak Teeth Filed Concavely.
(After Lieut. F. S. Marryat.)

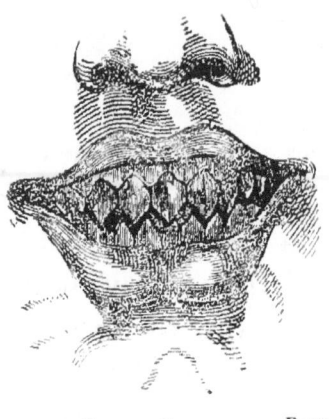

Dyak Teeth Filed to a Point.
(After Lieut. F. S. Marryat.)

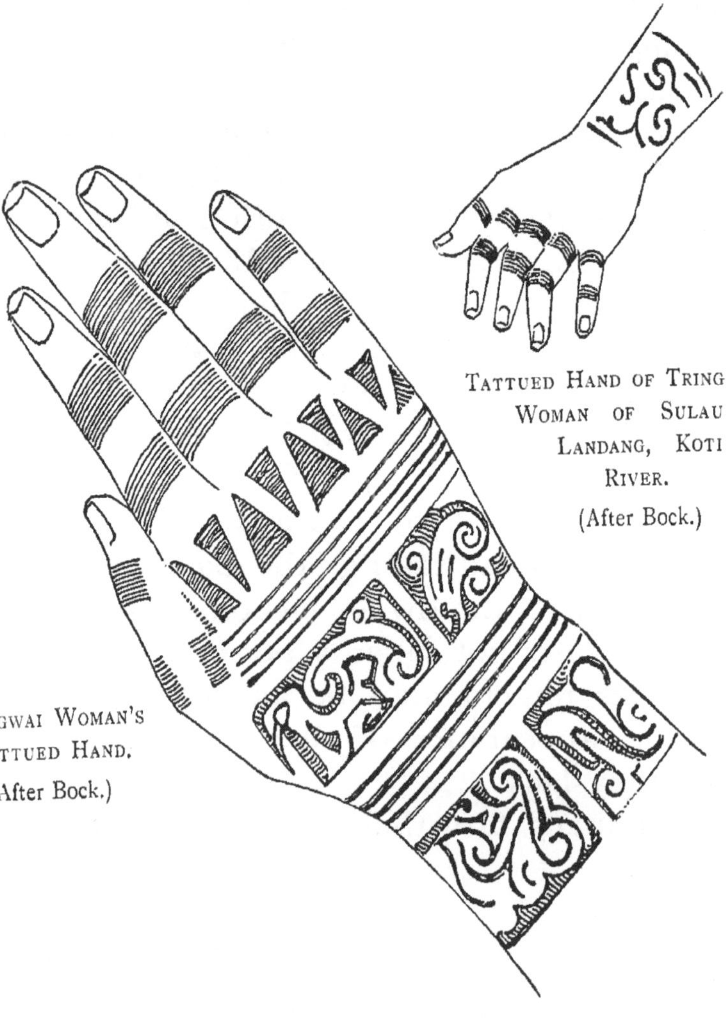

Tattued Hand of Tring Woman of Sulau Landang, Koti River.

(After Bock.)

Longwai Woman's Tattued Hand.

(After Bock.)

THE PEOPLE AND THEIR CUSTOMS 35

and the Milanaus simulate bracelets, necklaces and armlets. A Murut was found with two square marks on his back, denoting that he had shown his back to the enemy and run away in a fight.

Rising to clothes, the most general dress for men is the *chawat*, a strip of black or dark blue cloth, one yard wide and six to fourteen yards long, which they twist round and round their waists, leaving one end hanging down over it in front, and the other hanging like a tail behind. The rest of their dress consists of a bead necklace, and a black or blue head-cloth, brass wire bracelets, from the wrist to the elbow, and above that armlets of rattan or silver. The women wear a tight petticoat, barely reaching the knees and edged sometimes with silver coins; over it, round the waist, are coils of rattan dyed black, and belts made of silver coins. They wear armlets of tapang wood or of shell above the elbow, and brass rings from the wrist to the elbow and from ankle to knee. Sometimes to these ornaments is added a loose jacket, this and the petticoats being made of material woven and dyed by themselves. They grow the cotton which they beat out into strips; it is then spun on a quaint kind of spinning wheel, and woven on primitive looms, one kind worked by hand, another by treadles as well. The designs and combinations of colour are extremely good; sometimes a pattern is worked on the cloth, or a worked piece put over the plain as a border or a yoke, but the women also make the design in a curious way as they weave. They sketch the pattern out on the web; they then pick up all over the loom the threads which are to be of certain colours, perhaps red and yellow, and cover them closely with vegetable fibre, leaving only threads which are to be blue exposed; the whole is then dipped into a blue dye; when it is dry the vegetable covering is cut off and the same process gone over with the other colours; after this it is woven with a light brown weft. The shuttles are beautifully ornamented, the white wood being stained a rich red in a pattern covering the whole shuttle. Instead of cotton, lengths of fibre which run along the under side of the *limba* leaf are much used for cloth as it is easier to weave.

The Dusun women wear larger petticoats dyed indigo; over them are coils of black and red rattan to support their petticoats, and hanging from these are rows of red beads and brass chains.

In many of the tribes the women wear a curious bodice arrangement called a *saladan*. This is made of bamboo split, pared thin, flattened and dyed black; it is fitted on to the body, and kept in position by brass wires about an inch apart; children are caged in this armour, which is only removed as they outgrow it. The Ulu Ai women have eight

Dyak Girl Weaving.

or ten rows of large brass rings threaded on rattan fixed on a cane framework round their bodies; it is secured down the front by a vertical bar, curved outwards on one side and inwards on the other to form a fastening; others again wear brass wires wound round them horizontally, continued from the waist right up under the arms, and the Land-Dyaks have brass wire "corsets" of the same kind but arranged perpendicularly. Thin hoops of crimson cane are worn by others.

Beads are very popular, and are worn by both men and women as necklaces, and by women strung in many rows as girdles and hip laces. Mixed with the beads are various stones of considerable value: one hip lace was valued at £35. Dresses of strings of shells, beads and polished stones are costly too, and make a sound as of bells as the wearer walks. Expensive also are the necklaces of bears' teeth, of which forty may be used for one person.

In one tribe both men and women wear rain mats folded up into a basket on their back, whence the rain mat is taken out and thrown over the head in wet weather.

The men wear mat-seats tied on behind, shaped like a shield, so that they always have a dry seat. They are made either of a bear's or panther's skin, or of cane woven in patterns with cowrie shells, buttons or beads introduced. Monkeys are used for food, and their skins are worn with the tail hanging down behind.

Pieces of black or blue cloth are twisted into head dresses, but the very beautiful plaiting of coloured rattans is used for caps and hats of all shapes and sizes, wonderful plumes of feathers standing up from the centre.

The ears are objects of much adornment. Fifteen to twenty ear-rings are worn in as many holes pierced along the rim of the ear, and are of great size and weight.

The bark of trees provides material for chawats and petticoats for many of the poorer Dyaks. Long, thin, round beaters, grooved at intervals, are used to beat out the bark till it is thin and soft enough to be fashioned, and it can be beaten so fine that mosquito curtains were formerly made of it.

All primitive races have primitive ways of obtaining fire, a universal necessity. The Dyaks used to get it by means of fire syringes. A cylinder of metal, lead and tin mixed, was cast in a bamboo mould, into this a bit of tinder, made from the stem of a palm, was driven down in the hollowed end of a wooden piston, and a smart knock on the piston set light to the tinder. There are also ruder forms of fire sticks, in which fire is obtained by friction; but a large number of Dyaks now use matches, bought by barter from the Chinese.

SEA-DYAKS WITH SEAT MATS.

Two chief occupations of the women are to bring down from the loft, where it is piled up by the men, sufficient wood for the daily need, and to pound the paddy (or rice). Rice is the staple food of the people. Since there is no dearth of land, the Hill-Dyaks generally plant one crop of rice, the next year sugar-cane, and then leave their land fallow for eight or ten years, while they move on to new ground. The seed is saved with great care, and sown in holes fifteen to eighteen inches apart; after a time the field is most carefully weeded with a sort of spud. In March or April the paddy becomes a rich gold colour which tells that the crop is ripe. Then a picturesque scene takes place. The men, with a basket tied on them in front, and holding a small, oddly shaped knife, go between the rows and cut off the heads one by one, for the whole does not ripen at once; these are worked to and fro over a square sieve of rattan fixed between four posts, and the paddy which falls through is stored in the roof of the houses. Part of the women's duty is to husk enough of this for the day; they have pestles five feet long and very thin; two women use each a pestle in one mortar, cut out of the trunk of a tree, till the rice is all freed from the husk and is quite white and ready for use. With the rice, fish, fowls, pork, venison, vegetables and fruit are used for food. Their cooking is cleanly, for, except for boiling rice, which is done in brass pots, they use cooking vessels made of bamboo, which are thrown away after using. At their meals leaves or plates hold the rice, but forks or spoons, or even chopsticks, are not the "mode," and everything is eaten with the fingers.

The languages used by all the tribes seem to belong to the Malay family, and many words are taken directly from the Malay, but there are differences which render it impossible for one tribe to understand another. One peculiarity among some of the Dyaks is that they cannot pronounce the letter L, for which they use R.

A curious custom prevails as to personal names. Instead of the northern method of designating a son by his father's name, *e.g.*, William John-son, the Dyaks reverse the order and the father takes the name of his son or grandson. So a man Jan, who has a son Laking, changes his name to Apai Laking (father of Laking), and if a grandchild is called Ngipa, the grandfather becomes Aki Ngipa.

Tribes do not intermarry much, and in the same tribe prohibited degrees are very carefully kept, marriage between first cousins not being allowed. Polygamy, though by some tribes not forbidden, is rarely practised, but a wife is often divorced, sometimes because the omen of the unlucky cry of a deer or a bird has been heard. The wedding feast takes

THE PEOPLE AND THEIR CUSTOMS 41

place at the family house which the bride or the bridegroom is to leave; if the couple are to live with the man's people, the festivities are at the bride's house and *vice versa*. As a rule, daughters are considered more valuable than sons, because a father with several girls to marry can get so many sons-in-law to live in his house and to work for him, whereas the sons may be taken off to their brides' houses. Which side they shall live with is, however, a matter of arrangement.

At the marriage feast the company assemble on the *ruai*; betel-nut is provided for the general chewing, and besides this one or two nuts are split into eight pieces and placed on a plate with pieces of gum and lime; these represent the bridegroom's responsibilities. Seven other pieces of betel-nut are then placed on the same plate on the bride's side; the plate is left on the verandah covered over with a red cloth. Two pieces of bamboo are split, one into eight, the other into seven, tied together with red thread and hung up over the hearthstone in the verandah. After this a marriage contract is pronounced, setting forth that if either man or woman desert the other without sufficient cause they shall pay a fine, in jars, of such relative value as is agreed on. Two plates equal one irun, two iruns one menkul, two menkuls one jabir, two jabirs one pandung, two pandungs one alas; one of these is chosen as the

" value " according to the position of the people, and that, multiplied by the number of pieces of betel by which they are represented on the plate when it is uncovered, determines the fine to be paid. As the value of one plate is three or four pence an alas is worth 10s. 8d., and the husband's highest fine would be the serious sum (in jars) of £4 5s. 8d. If the same number of pieces are found on the plate when it is uncovered as were put there, a life free from extremes of happiness or sorrow is to be foretold for the couple; if the *antus* have stolen away any pieces there will be sorrow, and if more pieces have been added it bodes great good fortune.

When the bride goes to visit her husband's house she is so heavily weighted with ornaments of brass rings, ear-rings, necklaces and silver coins and hawks-bells hanging from her skirts that she can hardly move. For three days and nights in one house, and then in the other, whichever the newly married pair are staying in, a deafening sound of drums and gongs is kept up, so that no evil omens may be heard. To each house they carry with them pulut (cooked rice) and cakes, of which they invite the inmates to partake. Live fowls are whirled seven times round the bridegroom's head, then killed, and the blood sprinkled on the foreheads of the couple while a blessing is invoked.

Before a child is born a *tabu* is imposed on both

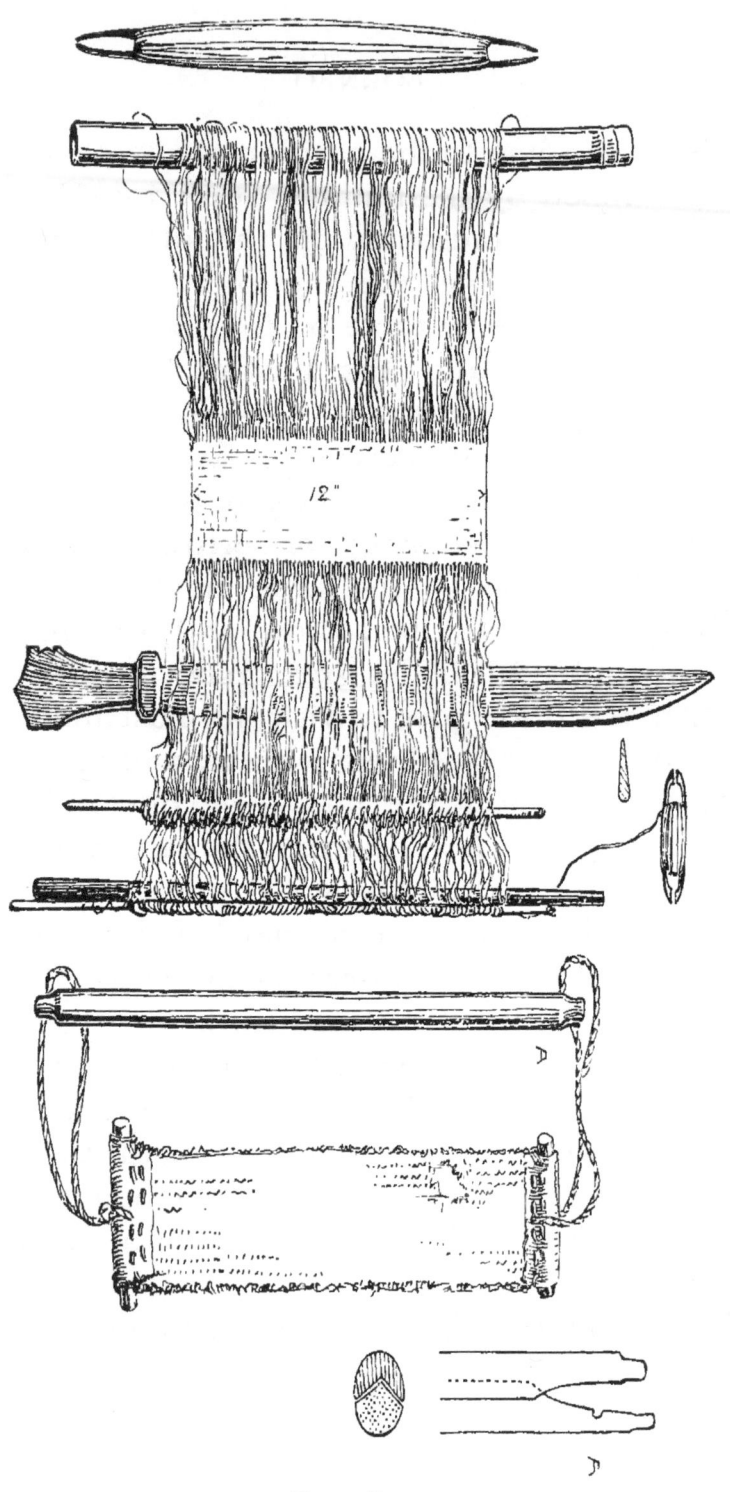

Dusun Loom.
(Brit. Mus.)

THE PEOPLE AND THEIR CUSTOMS 43

the father and mother. Neither of them may handle cloth or cotton, or take hold of a chopper; they may not tie anything (*e.g.*, as a string round a post) nor let fall a stone. No plaiting of basket work or mat work may be begun, and no animal, wild or tame, be killed. Should the father kill anything out hunting some one else must claim it as his, to avert the evil.

The Land-Dyaks have so much land to choose from that, with clearly defined boundaries, the land belongs to the tribe and there is little individual tenure, though for convenience some plots near to the village are allotted to certain families for paddy fields, and on the owner's death are divided equally between his children. Among the Sea-Dyaks the man who cleared a piece of land from its forest growth was held to be the owner of it, with power to sell or let it at a rent not exceeding one dollar, but now that the value of land is rising this rent is raised too.

Fruit, bamboo and other trees belong to individuals, but there are frequent disputes about fruit-tree rights, and fallen fruit is common property. It has been said that the Dyaks are so honest that they never think of gathering the fruit of a tree belonging to some one else.

These races of differing habits, customs, natures, what ideal is to be set before them, and what contribution shall they make to the great building of the Church?

The Malay, "Nature's gentleman" as he has been called, proud of his ancient race, polite, daring and adventurous, has sunk from his high estate. What shall he bring? Perhaps, through the faith of Islam, the consciousness and the open acknowledgment of God's Presence, and the courage in peril which should make him strong for Christ, but among these people the Church in Borneo cannot work as yet; a field more than large enough lies outside them.

The Chinese, industrious, reliable, capable, have given no uncertain proof of the steadfastness they can show even unto death, of their wonderful power as evangelisers, of the practical surrender of their lives to be changed by the power of the Holy Spirit, and of their sense of the unity of the Church.

The Dyaks surely, in their tribal communities, must have been prepared to grasp very fully the doctrine of the corporate life of the Church. Races, childlike in their primitive conditions, ignorant perhaps of truth, but docile, gentle, pre-eminently honest as regards the property of others, they offer a splendid character as their contribution, a field prepared for the seed by their realisation of the unseen, a realisation now in the form of a world of good and evil spirits around them, but only waiting to be quickened by the breath of life into communion with Him whom we may declare unto them. Down-trodden and oppressed as they were for centuries, with what a revelation must it come to them that the great All-Father loves them and wants their love. Only the ideal that, weak as they are, yet He deems them worthy of His love, can raise them so that all may be one in Christ Jesus, that they may look up to Him as the Head of the Church, of which they all are members, Dyaks, Kayans, Muruts, Hakkas, Foo-kins, all baptised unto the one Body, all strengthened by the one Bread, all walking in the Spirit, through Whom they shall grow up into Him " from Whom the whole body, fitly joined together and compacted by that which every joint supplieth, maketh increase of the body unto the edifying of itself in love ".

QUESTIONS ON CHAPTER II

1. What do you know about the Malays?
2. Have the Chinese any particular qualities which fit them for opening out new tracts of land?
3. Describe a " village " of Sea-Dyaks.
4. What preliminaries are observed when they want to migrate to a new home?
5. What system of internal government is observed by the Land-Dyaks?
6. How do the women chiefly pass their time, and

have they any particular modes of dress, or personal habits?

7. Have the Dyaks any marriage laws, or any peculiar wedding customs?

8. What is there worthy of being contributed to the building up of the Church in (*a*) the Malay character, (*b*) in the Chinese, (*c*) in the Dyak?

CHAPTER III

The People, Feuds, War and Death

WE saw in the last chapter that the dwellings of many tribes were built "high" and "long" to ensure safety. Constant feuds between the races, attacks sudden and unlooked for, kept them always on the defensive. But besides attacks due to old tribal quarrels there was the "national" custom of head-hunting, which might bring an invader any day simply because he wanted to win a bride—not to carry one off, but to win the trophy which would gain for him the favour of his chosen one. Ghastly it seems to us that a human head, or heads, should be the love-charm without which no Dyak in old days could presume to hope for the acceptance of his addresses, yet, maybe, it was only carrying out into a gross realism and "evidence" the spirit of the days of chivalry when fair ladies smiled on the victor who overthrew his rival in the lists. It gives us at any rate the measure of the Dyak's value of human life.

To him human life has no sacredness; he knows

nothing of the Maker in Whose image man was made, he knows not that the breath of life was breathed into him by God Himself, a trust to be guarded and used for His glory.

The practice of head-hunting is very ancient ; possibly it originated in the idea of a votive offering to the evil spirits, an idea which still exists, for not only is a head necessary as a love offering, but at the feasts held to propitiate the spirits of fertility, that they may give abundant crops to the ground, a newly killed head must be present, and the earth must be sprinkled with the water in which the head has been washed. The spirits of sickness, too, must be appeased in the same way, and the dead remain unburied until a head can be procured. There is a dumb instinct that in some way the shedding of blood is needed ; they wait to learn, through us, that not sickness, not famine, are the true evils, but sin, for which, without shedding of blood, there is no remission, and that only the sacrifice of love upon the Cross can bring to them pardon and peace.

As in so many things, the tribes vary in their customs in disposing of the heads. The Sea-Dyaks, as we saw, hang them up over the fireplace in the *ruai*, or else they tie them up in rattan and string them in festoons. The Kayans do the same, but they carve the skull with elaborate patterns deeply incised into it ; the heads are smoked over a wood

SEA-DYAK CHIEF, WITH HEADS.

fire, and when they are not carved the hair and teeth are preserved, and make them look even more horrible.

The Land-Dyaks build a separate round or octagonal house for their heads, and each village has always one such house, often two or three. This *pangah* is raised on posts, and sometimes the entrance is by a trap-door in the floor; the house serves a double purpose; first it is a storehouse for the heads, which are ranged round the steeply conical roof inside, or hung from beams by strings passed through the top of the skulls, so that they swing about and knock against each other in a wind, and then, too, it serves as quarters for all the unmarried men of the village, and for strangers, who wake up to see the fitful light from the central fire casting weird gleams on the uncanny company above.

In some cases heads belong to the chief, or to the slayer who has brought them home in the head-basket worn at his side, in other cases to the tribe collectively; if, in a war waged jointly by two tribes on another, only one head should be taken, it is cleft in twain, and half belongs to each tribe. But to the man who has taken many heads belongs a pride of glory; he carries himself with assurance as a "brave" before his chief, and he only is allowed to wear, pierced through the top of each ear, the tooth of the Borneo leopard-cat.

The reception of heads in a village is an occasion of many ceremonies; they may have food, sirih or betel-nut placed in their mouths, and be carried in procession; feasts are held, trophy poles raised up and pigs and fowls killed.

Of course the whole custom of head-hunting was dealt with by Sir James Brooke, and has been in great measure suppressed. The present Rajah wrote: "As soon as ever one of these (head-hunting) parties started, or even listened to birds of omen preparatory to moving, a party was immediately despatched by Government to endeavour to cut them off, and to fine them heavily on their return, or, in the event of their bringing heads, to demand the delivering up of them, and the payment of a fine into the bargain. This was the steady and unflinching work of years, but before many months were over my stock of heads became numerous, and the fines considerable. Some refused to pay or follow the directions of the Government, these were declared enemies, and had their houses burnt down forthwith, and the people who followed me to do the work would be the Dyaks of some other branch tribe on the same river."

Head-hunting, of ancient use among the land tribes, was greatly fostered when some of the Sea-Dyak tribes were drawn into piracy. The Malays and Lanuns were pirates of the worst type. In the

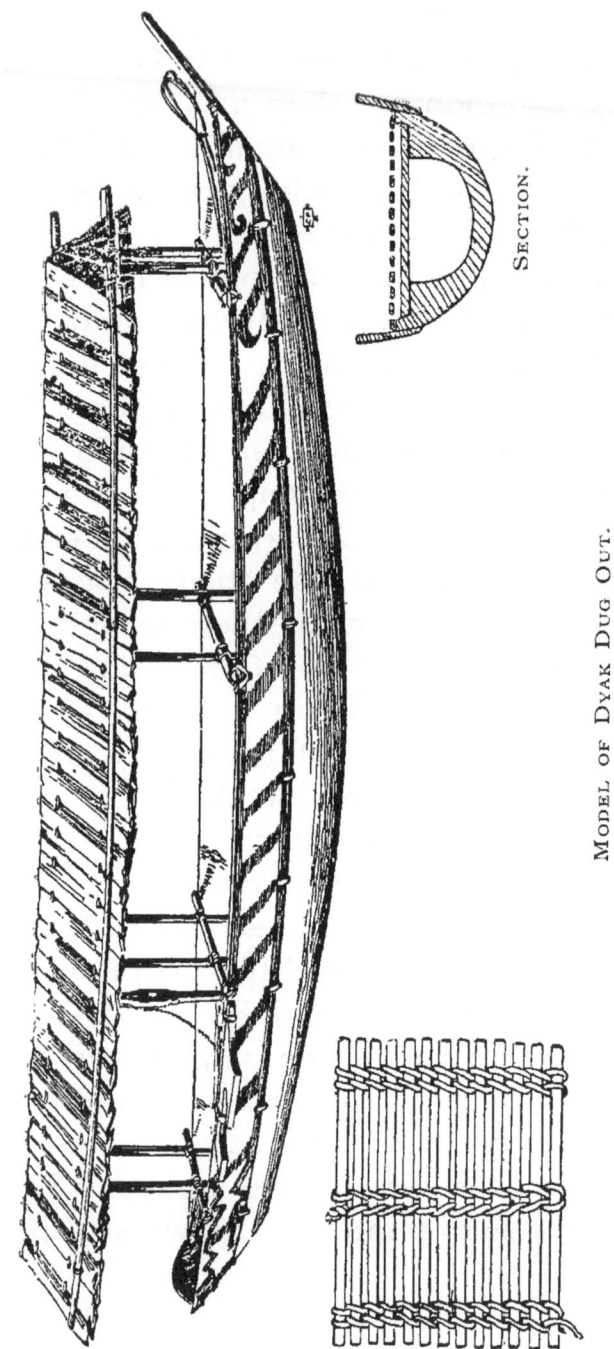

Model of Dyak Dug Out.
(Leggatt Coll.)

Section.

THE PEOPLE, FEUDS, WAR AND DEATH 51

Malay *prahus*, long boats, manned by thirty to forty rowers, with a flat roof from which the warriors fought, the Dyaks were found useful in the marauding expeditions, and their help was secured by giving them the heads of the killed, while the Malays took the plunder for themselves, and the captives for their slaves.

The *bankongs*, the Dyak boats, were larger than the *prahus*, some holding seventy or eighty men; they, too, had a flat roof on which the fighting men stood, while their comrades paddled below, a white shell bracelet marking each dark arm along the edge of the boat, as they pulled all together in measured stroke, the chief standing astern to steer. If they landed, a hut was built and each man slept, sword and shield in hand ready to spring upon the slightest alarm. The Kayans even strewed dead leaves around outside their huts so that any footfall might be heard.

Curious to us are the Balau boats, which have no nails but are simply lashed together with rattan; the keel has a ledge on each side, inside the margin, on which the edge of the next plank is rested; holes are pierced through and laced with rattan; each plank in its turn has a ledge on which the one above is placed, and so the boat is built up. If a landing is to be made, or when the expedition is over, the boat is unlashed, and laid up as a pile of planks. As a Dyak said to Sir Charles Brooke: " Tuan, our (boats) are regulated for land, and there we beat yours, for we can walk away with ours and build them again in any other direction in the rivers on the other side of the mountains ".

For these *bankongs* the useful nipa-palm again comes in: awnings (*kadjang*) are made of it, like the house roofs, in sections of six feet and a half square; folded in half they are easily rolled up and stowed away, or if opened partly out they form a tent-like roof. No oars or sails are used, only paddles, but each tribe has its own particular stroke, so that they can tell in the dark, by sound alone, whether friend or foe is coming. So strong are the boats and so enduring the men, that these *bankongs* used to be met with forty miles down the coast, until piracy was to a great extent put down. The paddles are most gracefully shaped, and the handles sometimes carved and inlaid with silver.

The war dress is a quilted jacket, covered sometimes by a goat skin, slit above the shoulders for the man's head to go through, so that the goat's head hangs down in front as a protection, and the back covers the wearer's shoulders. On their heads they wear a basket helmet covered with skins or metal plates. The only real defence is the shield of various shapes, generally oblong and convex, made of light wood and beautifully carved, with

KAYAN SHIELD.

FRONT. BACK.

From Sarawak. On the front along the median ridge there is a rib of iron twisted at both ends. Decorated with human hair. Length, 40½ ins. (Edinbro' Mus.)

a handle held by the left hand. The arms are: the spear, made of bilian wood with a steel point, which is used in close combat; the lance, also of hard wood, the point hardened in the fire; this is thrown at the enemy before he is near enough for the spear to be used; then there is the *parang* (sword) made in different shapes; some are curved, but not, like a scimitar, from the hilt; the upper part is straight, and only the end is curved. These weapons are also much used for clearing and other jungle work.

The Kayans used to smelt their own ore, and though this is not done so much now, they still excel in ironwork and in the temper of their weapons. Some of these cost as much as £10, and one kind, a curious short sword, having convex and concave blades, is a treasure coveted by every Dyak boy.

But the most destructive weapon is the *sumpitan*, a blow-pipe, through which the natives project poisonous arrows. This is a tube six to eight feet long, made of dark red wood. A perfectly straight hole is drilled up the centre by an iron rod, made of the fine Kayan metal, and pointed like a chisel at one end. The exact evenness of the bore surprises those who see the means used, for the length of wood is simply fixed to one of the house posts, and the workman, standing below, bores his hole upwards. Afterwards the bore is smoothed down inside by a piece of rattan drawn up and down, and when that is finished the wood is pared down outside to an inch in diameter, polished and ornamented with a pattern inlaid with tinfoil. The arrows used are slips of nibong palm pointed, and their tips hardened in the fire and fitted with a small butt of light wood or dried pith; they are nine to twelve inches long and extremely light. Those used in war have a loose barbed point of tin or bamboo, which is dipped in poison and remains in the wound. Very elegant quivers are made of bamboo, carved and painted or finished by rings of coloured rattan with shells embedded in a layer of gutta-percha; they have a long hook by which they are hung from the belt on the left side; in war they are kept open so that the arrows can be easily reached, but the Kayans often hold four spare arrows between their fingers and will shoot them five times as quickly as a musket could be fired. They use the sumpitan, of course, raised to the mouth, and can hit at a range of a hundred yards; at sixty yards the force of their "blow" is sufficient to kill a monkey, and at twenty yards to send the arrow half its length into the enemy's flesh.

The poison is got from the *upas* tree, in which incisions are made, and through them the poisonous gum is collected; this is heated over a fire till it becomes like thick wax, and is then spread on a plate and the arrow-heads rolled in it. Some of the

BAMBU QUIVER

(S.E. Coast.)

Bands on upper portion are dark brown and yellow rotan. The two ends of the quiver painted dark crimson. The belt hook is of iron. (Brit. Mus.)

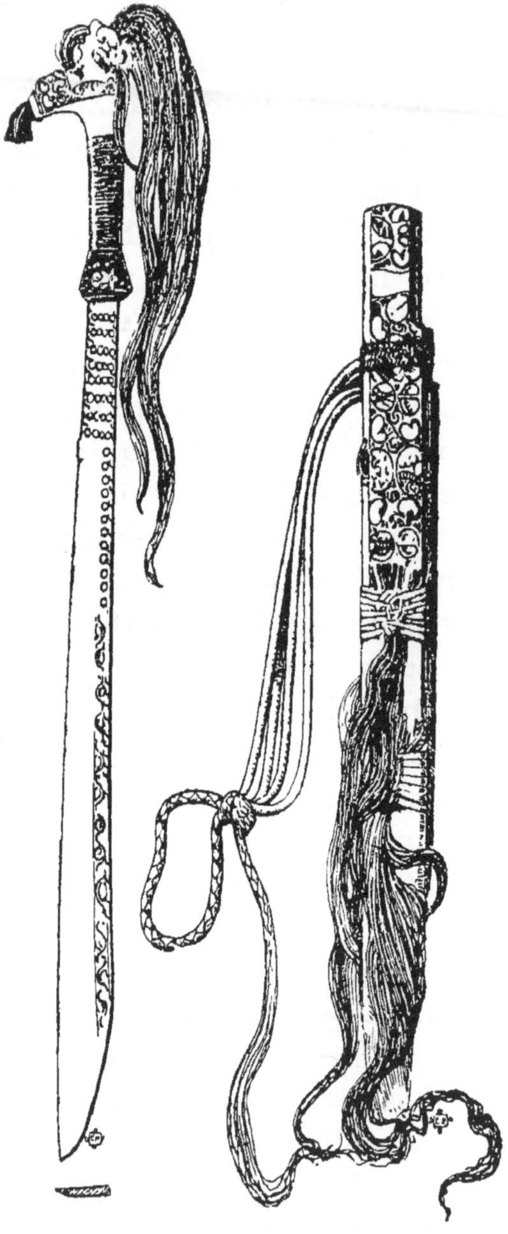

PARANG ILANG.

With wooden sheath. The blade chased and pierced, the hilt of carved ivory (?) with inserted tufts of hair. (Dublin Mus.)

natives carry a box of lime juice, into which they dip the arrows just before shooting in order to make the poison more virulent. A poison obtained from the *ipoh* tree is also used; in both the active agent is strychnine, which acts upon the heart and the spinal cord. According to the freshness or strength of the poison the person or animal hit may die in a few minutes, in some hours, or may only become feverish and ill; but in any case no outward sign is observed beyond a tiny prick where the arrow has pierced the skin.

The Dyak's absolute belief in the spirit world gives him the explanation of all sickness. In some way or other it is the work of the *antus*, the evil spirits who are so real to him. Either the spirit has struck the man, or has come into him and taken possession of him, or else it has enticed his soul away out of his body. There must, therefore, be two distinct courses of treatment, one to drive away the invading spirit, the other to capture and bring back the wandering one. For either of these only the medicine men and women can avail. The medicine men, among the Land-Dyaks, are called *daya bururi ;* their office is sometimes, but not generally, hereditary and they rank as priests. They claim to be able to see the spirits and so can recognise the vagrant soul, and rescue it from the clutches of the malignant spirits. They seldom give medicine internally, so perhaps the treatment does less harm than might be expected, though the noise, which seems a necessary part of it, would kill most Europeans.

If the patient does not recover after local applications of curious messes, such as pepper, chilis, fowl's blood and turmeric, or after the part affected has been stroked with a charm, out of which come pieces of stone, wood and cloths which the charm has extracted from the body, two treatments are offered:—

1. *Punja.*—For this a pig and a fowl are killed; portions of these animals with rice and betel-nut are placed in a paddy shovel outside the door, so that the *antus* may feast and depart; the house is under *tabu* or *pemali*, no stranger may come in; the family may not go out of their room for four days, and the *daya* and four medicine women must be in attendance; the man beats a drum, and two of the women have a fierce fight outside the door. Singing and beating of drums and gongs goes on for two days; then at midnight the *daya* wraps up a cup in a white cloth and places it amidst the offering provided for the spirits; he waves his charm and a torch wildly about and calls on someone to look into the cup; there, to ordinary eyes, surely enough is a bunch of hair, but this the *daya* declares to be the recovered soul, which is then put

Preparing Poison for Darts.

back into the sick man's body through an imaginary hole in his skull, though there is no promise that it will not wander forth again. On the last day a chicken is wrapped up in the outer leaf of a pinang blossom, covered with red cloth, carried to a stream at some distance and let loose. If the bird returns to the village the patient may die, if it runs away into the jungle he may recover.

For the second treatment, *Sesab*, the house is *tabu* for eight days; the same animals are killed, and food provided for the *antus* on a bamboo altar; a continued tomtom of drums is kept up, and a wild dance carried on; the soul is said to be caught as in the other " treatment," and the man is washed in cocoa-nut water—a wholesome improvement on the general method which forbids washing or fresh air.

The medicine men of the Sea-Dyaks are called *manang* and hold very high rank, often becoming village chiefs. By the supernatural powers which they claim the people are kept in great awe of them, and they take good care to be well paid, and to feast plentifully during their stay at a house. They are supposed to have a good spirit always in attendance on them, and the cure of the patient depends on whether this good spirit or the sufferer's evil one is the stronger. The *manang* is very cunning, and besides herbs he often uses medicines which he has got from the Government dispensary. To cure pain, like the Land-Dyak *dayas*, he applies charms, and by sleight of hand pretends to bring some object, a ball of moss, a bone or rag, which he says has caused the pain, out of the body. They have also magic stones, quartz crystals into which they gaze to discover the reason of the ailing man's sickness.

The *manang's* degree is conferred on him by other *manang* in mystic ceremonies, described to the people as cutting open his head, taking out and washing the brains to give him clearness of insight, putting gold-dust into his eyes to enable them to see the soul, and fastening barbed hooks on to the end of his fingers by which he may catch it and hold it fast.

The sufferings of these poor people, deafened in their pain by beating of drums, swung sometimes violently to and fro for hours, stifled by bad air and crowded rooms, must surely appeal to us to give them physical relief by means of mission hospitals and dispensaries, and through these to bring them to the knowledge of the love of the Great Physician who went about healing those possessed of devils.

When the medicine man has failed and the person dies, among the Land-Dyaks the body is burnt, by some tribes in all cases; by others only in those of rich people; the bodies of the poorer classes being either buried in the earth, or placed

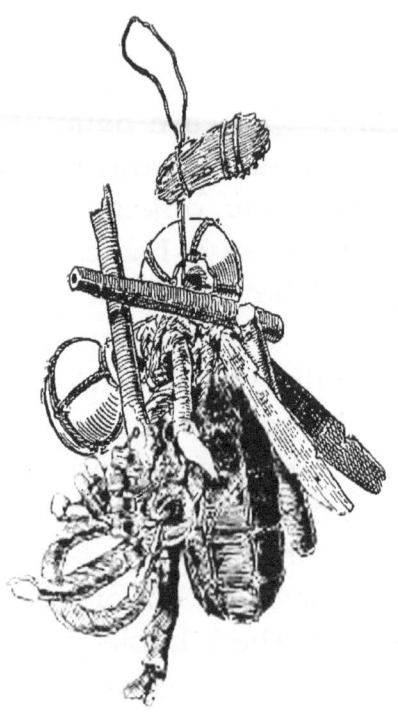

BUNDLE OF CHARMS,

Consisting of bits of wood, two Chinese celadons, beads, bast and a packet of cotton. Some of the wood cut head-shaped. From S.E. Borneo.
(Leiden Mus.)

VASE, CHINESE.

SUMPITAN.

Pattern inlaid with tin foil. Length, $80\frac{3}{8}$ in., bore, $\frac{7}{10}$ in., weight, 29 oz.
(Oxford Mus.)

on a covered stage erected for them, or rolled in a mat and carried out into the jungle. There is a great reluctance to perform the function of burning, and it is difficult to get any one to undertake the office of sexton. This man carries the corpse out of the village, followed part of the way by wailing women; at the burying-place a pile of wood is arranged, which surrounds and covers the body; wood, cloth, food, and sometimes a head, are laid beside it, and then the whole is set fire to.

The Sea-Dyaks bury their dead; the body is dressed in its best, and, in the case of a man, the arms and war weapons are laid upon it; it is then rolled up in mats tied together by rattan and taken to the burial-ground. The graves are very shallow, for the people will not get into them in making lest they should, later, die a violent death; they use no spades, but kneel or lie on the edge, cut the soil with a chopper, and throw it out with their hands; in this way they can only reach down two or three feet. Before they begin to make the grave they must kill a fowl and sprinkle the blood on the ground and on the feet of the dead man. The grave is covered by sticks eighteen or twenty-four inches high, kept in place by cross pieces of wood, and the coffin is formed simply of the trunk of a tree split in half.

Belief in some future state leads the friends to place articles of food and clothing in the grave, and outside it they leave some attributes denoting the former calling of the deceased. A warrior's grave will be marked by some of his arms, that of a hunter by some trophies of the chase, tusks or antlers, his sumpitan and arrows, while a woman's grave will be shown by a spindle or a water gourd.

When a Sea-Dyak child dies the body is put into a jar. Among those who have become Christians, and whose children are baptised, the jars are buried in the earth, but a jar holding an unbaptised child is not buried but is hung up on the branch of a tree, perhaps a fruit-tree !

The Kayans, like the Sea-Dyaks, bury their dead, but first the man is dressed in his finest clothes, seated upright on his mat, with a cigarette held to his mouth, and a betel box by his side, his friends sit round the room and talk to him, giving him instruction as to the road he should take. After a feast has been held the body is put into a coffin, and carried in procession to a high pole or tree on which it is raised ; the man is told to go straight on when he comes to three roads, as the right one leads to Borneo, the left to the sea, but the centre one to his own country.

Bishop McDougall thus describes a funeral among the Milanaus : " The women kept up dismal weepings during the night. In the morning I went to

Milanau Grave.

see the young chief's things laid out preparatory to their being sent on their further journey after him. They were all arranged under a canopy made of his *sarongs*. Two [of these] were of rich gold cloth (value about fifty dollars each), and the rest of his wardrobe was disposed under it, so as to represent a corpse on a bier, the gold ornaments alone, consisting of large buttons, a breastplate, and a very rich and handsome *kris* handle of ancient Japanese and Indian manufacture representing a figure of Buddha, cannot be worth less than 200 dollars; besides this there were gongs, and two brass guns. Two women were lying by the bier, on either side the effigy, and the father (a very old man) sat beside it watching, the women every now and then raising a mournful howl. In three days these things will be launched down the river in a boat made for the purpose, and if any one were known to touch it he would be slain. If the body had been recovered it would have been launched with its former property in the boat. This is the invariable mode of burial with the Milanaus. The general fate of these funeral boats is to get capsized, when the things all go to the bottom."

The Kanowits also build "soul-boats," in which some of the dead man's property, and sometimes a slave, is sent adrift that he may have them to help him on his way.

Launching these "soul-boats" reminds one of the

beautiful floating away of the old Vikings, lying in state in their high-prowed boats.

Elaborately carved houses called *salongs* with quaint roofs are raised by the Kayans to contain the coffins of their chief men and their relatives. One is described as having three rows of posts, three in each row; the two end ones going up to the pointed roof were twenty-six feet high, the others twenty-three feet; the room enclosed by them was thirteen feet by twelve feet; this contained four coffins, and the walls were lined by shields and paddles. Below the floor of the room, on shelves, rested the bodies of slaves or others belonging to the tribe, and there, too, was the chief's war-boat. The house was built of bilian wood. The sloping roofs are made sometimes of branches of the sago palm, and the gables are decorated with painted strips of bark. An old custom was to drive the largest post in these houses into the ground through the body of a living slave.

The Sea-Dyaks raise single or double round pillars, *klierings*, deeply carved all the way up, and having niches for the bodies of slaves and a hollow at the top to receive a jar holding the bones of the chief. This is covered by a square slab of stone. One very fine *kliering* is mentioned as thirty-two feet high; one pillar of this was four feet seven inches round, and the other seven feet.

MODEL OF KAYAN SALONG,
Or Burial Chamber of Ironwood.
(Brooke Low Coll.)

SKAPAN.
Kliering.

Or double pillar, carved and capped with stone slab covering the mortuary chamber in the hollow top.
(Brooke Low Coll.)

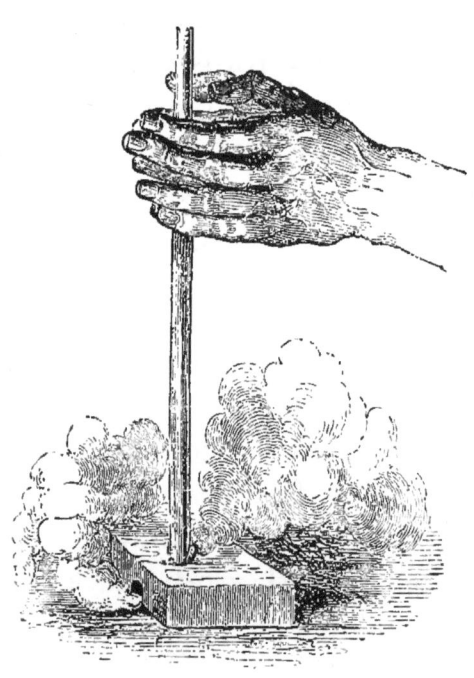

FIRE-DRILL (MARRYAT).
From *Natives of Sarawak*.

Among the Dusuns there is a custom which recalls one of which our ancestors left us traces. They mark the place where their warriors fell by a stone circle, a cross stone on the top of one slab representing the chief.

The Muruts have a horrible custom of doubling up their dead bodies and forcing them into jars, which, after a time, are buried.

Callousness in regard to human life was shown, as well as in head-hunting, in the sacrifice of slaves, common in many tribes when a chief died, so that their spirits might wait on him in the other world. One curious account is given of the Ida'an, who think that to reach Paradise the dead pass over a long tree, a difficult task to accomplish safely unless a man is killed to help them.

What an extraordinarily mixed population we see, then, in Sarawak alone, of many native races, of Chinese, Malays and Indians, with no national bond of union, no uniting force save of that of their revered Western ruler. Amongst them, native blood feuds of generations, the number of heads owed by a tribe carefully reckoned up for years, and the debt watched for and if possible taken at last—an eye for an eye and a tooth for a tooth. The Government has laid down and enforced that this Old Testament morality is not what may be permitted, and the Dyak has to submit, but to him it meant justice, and his blind obedience wonders why his "right" is "wrong" in the eyes of the white man.

The Chinese and the Indian, brought in solely as traders and workers, come to make money, and have no common interest with the Dyaks, whom they look down on as wild and uncivilised, and the Malay looks down on them all.

Only one force can weld these divergent interests and races, as Dane and Saxon were welded into one nation under the Cross of Christ; that alone can bring Chinese and Malay, Murut and Dusun, to look each on each as brother in the great family of God.

At one time or another the Church has been brought into contact with the people here described, but her chief work has been amongst the Dyaks and Chinese. Alas! at present there is only one English priest in Sarawak and one in British North Borneo, so that work which flourished in the past has now almost died out. Thirty years ago there were more than twice the number of missionaries now at work. The rebuilding of the waste places cannot be done unless the mother Church realises her responsibility for these children of nature, but given men, money and prayer, they can be gathered in and built up into the One Body.

QUESTIONS ON CHAPTER III

1. Has the Dyak any conception of the sacredness of human life?

2. What was done with the "heads" won by Dyak warriors?

3. What do you know about (*a*) their boats, (*b*) their war-dress, (*c*) their blowpipes?

4. How does the Dyak's belief in a spirit world affect him in sickness?

5. What are the medicine men called amongst (*a*) the Land-Dyaks, (*b*) the Sea-Dyaks? Is their office held in veneration?

6. In what way are the dead treated?

7. What is the Kayan procedure after a death?

8. Suggest some of the blessings which might be hoped for if the Church of Christ were strong and vigorous in Borneo, and able to promote her work untiringly.

CHAPTER IV

Superstitions and Beliefs and their Effects

FOR the Dyak the sense of the supernatural is extremely keen, and its influence pervades every action of his daily life. The spirit world surrounds him on every side; its voices speaking to him point out where he should build his house, warn him whether he should turn back from an expedition, tell him when to plant his paddy.

It is the inarticulate longing for some one greater than himself; the seeking after (if haply he may find) some Power above humanity, the dim sense of a Deity with whom he seeks to hold communion, and from whom to obtain guidance. "God made us for Himself, and our hearts can find rest only in Him," this is as true of the oriental as of the Western races, so in his darkness the Dyak follows what he knows, groping blindly among the spirits, till out of our light we point him to the Light of the world "which lighteth every man".

As a child of Nature the Dyak knows no other than Nature worship, but that worship claims his very soul, and to it he renders full obedience. In us the voice of conscience is too often buried deep; our hearts are untrained to interpret its speaking, and if we do hear it feebly we are too prone to bury it again and not in simple faith to heed its behests. The Dyak hears what he believes to be the voice of leading and implicitly obeys. To him it is not the voice of conscience, for he has no sense of sin; it is the voice of guidance which shall lead him where he may escape danger, and obtain ease and prosperity.

There is no Dyak literature, therefore it is impossible to trace the growth of their superstitions which have been handed down by word of mouth. As one generation has passed them on to another, memories have failed or imagination has added to the story, and so various versions are found, but all through beliefs and superstitions there runs only the idea of propitiating or appeasing gods and spirits in order that they may avert danger or give good material gifts. Worship resolves itself into a species of bribery, so many meals of rice or fowls offered to the "*antus*" that they may cease to bring down sickness, or may give good crops of paddy. The native has no idea whatever of any influence on his own spirit; material good, what he can *get* is all, not what he can *be*. The growth of his own spirit, character, is an unknown vision, and all the unseen spirits around him have nothing to do with any moral development. He has only got so far as " Let us eat and drink, for to-morrow we die"; his spirit may live on to wander in the realms of air and to be born in other forms, but the end is extinction or dissipation into Nature.

The Land-Dyaks believe, and we may surely call it a belief, in four chief spirits.

Tupa, the creator, the life-giver, creator of all living things, creator and preserver, for he not only creates but preserves life. *Tenubi*, the creator and sustainer of the earth and of all inanimate creation, the god who gives crops and harvests and provides food. Some tribes seem to hold these two as but one deity, who made and watches over *all* creation.

The third spirit is *Iang*, the god of healing, who gave knowledge to a certain Barich, a priestess who imparts her lore to the medicine men and women.

Fourthly, *Jirong*, the destroyer, the angel of birth and of death, at whose suggestion man's nature, created immortal by Tupa, was given over to him for destruction by sickness, accident or war.

It has been suggested that Tenubi, Iang and Jirong correspond to the powers of the Hindu religion, Brahma, Vishnu and Siva, emanating from Tupa, the one god, as those do from Bram.

After these gods come the *Umot*, of whom there are five or six orders. *Komang* (whose ranks are joined by the spirits of brave men) and *Triu* are spirits who live on the hilltops and rejoice in death; they are present at head feasts, and their aid is asked to speed the success of snares set for animals. Other Umots, Sisé, Perusang and Pemback, are chiefly voracious, for their presence is made known by their coming to devour scraps of bread, paddy or cooked rice.

Thirdly, there are the *Mino*. Men who have died a natural death become simple *Minos*, but these, too, die, pass into Rubang Sabayan, the place of departed spirits, and become *bejawi*; after another death they become *begutur*, and at the end of that life the essence of their being enters into the trunks of trees, but they have no further personal existence.

The spirits of men who have died accidentally, or of those killed in battle, whose heads have been taken, become *Pajabun* and *Buan*; they live in the jungle and their object is to injure mankind. The *Buan* appear as headless men, and delight to steal away souls.

The Land-Dyaks have some sense of praying and will invoke the aid of spirits. At their harvest feasts the chief man of the village stands at the house door and throws some yellow rice out of a cup to the winds, telling it to appeal for him to the Sultan, to the Rajah, to the rajahs of the sun, of the moon, of the stars, of the seven stars, and to Tupa, that he may approach acceptably, have good luck and blessing, and especially asking of Tupa that "he may behold our feast, may help us all, may give us good luck and abundance of paddy and rice; we ask for fish, we ask for wild pigs, we ask for many children, we ask for fruit, we ask for bees".

Roughly carved wooden figures are sometimes put up holding short spears, that they may drive away evil spirits from the village, but these idols do not seem to be worshipped, or to be held as of much importance.

Ideas as to a future life differ among the tribes. Some think that the spirits of men go to the mountain tops, while those of women remain where their bodies were burnt, but that re-incarnation goes on for ever.

The Milanaus picture another world like this with plenty of sago plantations (their special industry), but think that after a long life in that world they will become worms and caterpillars in the forest.

The Kayans believe in one Supreme Being, Laki Tenangong, who cares for all souls, and that the future state is one of many habitations, some for the good, some for the evil; those who die a natural death go to Apa Leggan, those killed by accident or in battle to Long Julan and so on; they also hold

MILANAU SORCERER.

that after death the soul may enter into an animal or bird which haunts the grave of its former body.

The beliefs of the Sea-Dyaks are much wider and more complicated than those of the Land-Dyaks. Petara is the name of their deity, and far far back there would seem to have been a faith in one Almighty Power. Now, however, Petara denotes endless spirits: each man has his own Petara or guardian in the unseen world, and not only men, but the animal world and things in nature in all their forms, have each a special Petara. Archdeacon Perham thinks the word comes from the Hindu Avatara. One distinct trait is that these Petara are all benevolent beings, the preservers of men, and doing only good to mankind.

Among the Balaus children are committed to the care of the Petara by a ceremony called Besant. A sacrifice is offered by the *manang*, and then a very beautiful invocation is chanted, calling first on the king of all the gods to look, and then going through the names of Petara of various powers.

Seleledu, who has charge of the little hills, like top-knots of the *bejampong* bird.

Selingiling, who has charge of the twigs of the sega rotan.

Sengungong, who has charge of the full-grown knotted branches.

From the Pleiades, like the glistening patterns of the long-flowing turbans, looks Petara Guyah.

From the Milky Way, like golden rings of the nabau snake, Petara Radau is observing.

From the Rainbow, also beautiful in dying, like the feet of an opened box, Petara Menani is looking and bending.

From the Evening Star, as big as the bud of the red hibiscus, Petara Magu is looking.

These, with many others of the gods dwelling in the treetops and in the midst of the earth, are called upon.

A year after this first ceremony of asking the Petara to look on the child, a second invocation is made, when the gods are invited to come down to the house to partake of a feast.

Besides these all-pervading Petara, the Sea-Dyaks have three deities who may be considered as the gods of their race.

Salampandai is a female spirit who creates mankind. In obedience to Petara's command to make a man she fashioned first one of stone; this speechless being was rejected by Petara, as was an iron man, also speechless; then Salampandai brought one of clay who had the power of speaking and who was accepted, and ever since she has gone on making men of the same clay; she is represented on earth by a frog, an animal which, though seldom seen, is treated with great reverence, and to which sacrifice is offered if it should enter into a house.

Pulang Gaya is the god of the ground. He lives below the earth and is called up on special occasions, as at the beginning of the year's farm work, or when axes are to be sharpened, so that he may bless the whetstones. Dyaks have a great veneration for stones and rocks to which they ascribe special powers. The whetstones are ranged round the verandah of the house, and a procession walks round and round them chanting petitions to Pulang Gaya to bless them and to bring good luck.[1]

Singalang Burong is the Sea-Dyaks' god of war, and a feast is made to him after head-taking; he is also the guardian of brave men, and the god of bird-omens, the ancestor of the Dyaks who communicates with them through his sons-in-law, the birds.

Inferior to these Petara and to the three gods is a whole realm of *antus*, spirits good and evil, dream beings some of them, who reveal themselves, bring medicines to work magic charms, and give

[1] Tradition says that Pulang Gaya, one of three brothers, was lost, sought for in vain, and duly mourned. When the next season came for paddy sowing all the land cleared in the day was each night covered again with jungle. A careful watch convicted Pulang Gaya of doing the mischief; he claimed to be the adopted son of the god of the earth, and demanded yearly sacrifices before farming began as his rent, failing which he would destroy the paddy.

directions as to conduct in visions of the night. To obtain some special wish a custom called "nampok" is followed out to invoke the spirits. A man will go to the top of some hill and spend the night in solitary vigil, with the hope that a good *antu* will come and endow him with the gift of strength or bravery which he needs. This custom is used, too, to secure relief from illness. Some time since a man from the Rejang having tried several hills went to Lingga; on the mountain there he offered his sacrifice; he lay down beside his little offering to spend the night, was visited by an *antu* and came down quite cured.

The *antus* whose influence is most felt, however, are the evil ones who roam the jungle in various forms and keep the people in a state of abject terror. Girgasi is the chief of these demons, and to meet him is to be sure of death. Some of these spirits dwell in trees, and to cut down such a tree is to incur their vengeance. Illness is often attributed to the man having unknowingly done this. To find out if a tree is so possessed the test is made of striking an axe into it at sunset; if it remains in the tree in the morning there is no fear, but if it has fallen out the tree must be shunned as the abode of an *antu*.

Nearly every illness is put down to the action of these evil beings. Small-pox is the chief *antu*, and

KANOWIT.
(Sir Hugh Low Coll.)

cholera one of the next most powerful ones. These spirits of sickness are hungry spirits, and will come quickly up the rivers from the sea to devour their human prey unless sacrifice of food is offered to stop them and a white flag of truce set up.

These sacrifices are generally of rice, eggs, plantains, bananas, fruit and fowls; they are put either on a brass salver, or, if away from the house, an altar of sacrifice is put up, made of sticks fastened together with rattan, with a pent-roof of nipa leaves over it. The *antu* is supposed to come and partake of the offering; if not visible as a spirit the natives say that it comes in the form of a pig or a fowl; but even if the food remains apparently untouched, they say that only the husk is there and the invisible essence has been consumed by the invisible spirit.

Sacrifice to secure successful farming is an important act, and blood must be an essential element. As there are no larger animals, a fowl or a pig is killed and the blood sprinkled over the ground, or the dead bird waved in the air over the paddy field. Sacrifice for a person needs also the shedding of blood.

There is no priesthood. In illness sacrifice is offered by the medicine men, who are called priests, but in other cases the chief of the tribe, or some old man, is chosen to perform the rite.

The superstition of omens is one which keeps the Dyak in hourly fear. Animals, birds or insects may bring him the warning he dreads, but birds give the most important omens, and they have become an object of worship. The origin of this special veneration for birds is differently described. One legend says that long ago a Malay and a Dyak were swimming across a river. Each had a book with him; the Malay tied his in his turban, and, his head being kept out of the water, he carried the book dry and safe to the farther side. The Dyak fastened his book in his chawat, where it was washed by the river and swept away. In place of this lost book bird-omens were given to the Dyaks as a guide.

Another story tells how some Batang Lupar Dyaks made a feast and invited many guests. When they arrived they all proved to be strangers. Still the Dyaks received them and entertained them as friends. When the guests were departing they were asked whence they came, when they declared themselves to be Singalang Burong and his sons-in-law. Birds were their deputies here, and in recognition of the Dyaks' hospitality they were told to watch over and guide them.

A longer legend says that in the early ages a man called Siu wandering one day near the coast meets a beautiful Dyak woman, who offers to marry him. He demurs as he has lost his way, but she

Kayans in War Dress.

tells him she can conduct him home. Arrived there they find his people mourning him as lost, and in their rejoicing at his return no questions are asked about the bride. A son named Seraguntung is born and grows wonderfully; one day he has a violent fit of crying, and his mother, refusing to take him from his father, packs up her things and departs. Presently Siu and the boy set out to find her; night after night they shelter in the forest, and always a leaf is found close by holding milk for the child. Passing boats refuse to take them, but one morning, as they gaze at the sea, a huge spider rises out of it and leads them across it to a farther shore. There they find themselves in the house of Singalang Burong, and discover that Siu's wife was Singalang's niece, and one of his spirit birds. One day the whole party go out hunting with their dogs, no dog having been provided for Siu and his boy, though they are told that they will be killed if they do not bring home some prey. Seraguntung calls to him a thin, starved dog, which at once becomes fat and strong; they alone succeed in the chase and bring home a wild boar; the others try to kill it, but their spears glance off, and Seraguntung, with a knife of his mother's, strikes the pig, which instantly drops down dead. These and other wonderful feats cause him to be acknowledged as a true grandson of Singalang Burong's. One day when his grandfather is away the boy looks under his magic pillow and sees his father's home. After this the two want to return, but first they are taught how to fight, how to plant paddy, and watch and care for its growth; they learn how to catch fish and deer, and more than all they are initiated into the meaning of omens. Birds, they are told, represent Singalang Burong in this world, and through them he will speak to encourage and to warn them.

Yet another legend tells that a Dyak marrying a spirit (for in those days spirits were visible to mortals, and men and spirits were equal) their children were birds, who having been cared for by the Dyaks have ever since repaid them by their guidance.

But whatever the origin of the superstition the present bondage is only too certain. The Sea-Dyaks have seven omen-birds, bearing the names and possessing the spirits of the seven sons of Singalang Burong. Before any jungle land can be cleared for paddy-planting these omens must be consulted. The man watches till the Pleiades are high enough above the horizon and then he goes out to listen. He wants to hear the *nendak*, the *katupong*, the *burong malam* (an insect) and the *beragai*, one after the other in the above order and all on his *left*. When he has heard the first he breaks off some twig and takes it back to his house, and so

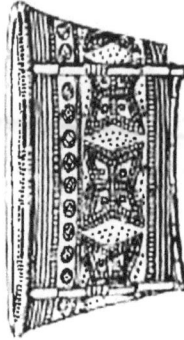

DIMINUTIVE MODEL OF DYAK HORN BILL.

With a Kembaian berry between its mandibles, a Monkey and two Squirrels on its tail.
(Brooke Low Coll.)

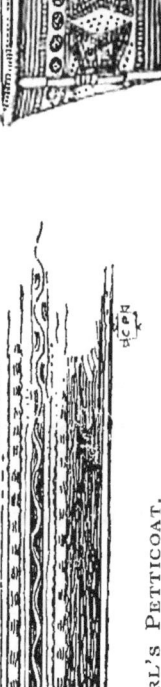

KANOWIT OPEN BASKET.
(Brooke Low Coll.)

PATTERN OF SEA-DYAK GIRL'S PETTICOAT.

With the exception of some red and yellow threads of warp along the edge which were dyed before putting on the loom, the pattern is dyed brown. Depth, 11 ins., circumference, 30 ins.
(Leggatt Coll.)

with the others, but if in between he hears some other bird he must begin all over again, and weeks may go by before the right succession is heard. Then the little twigs are taken to the ground and laid upon it, a prayer is offered to Pulang Gaya, and so the virtue of the birds is conveyed to the land.

Before a house can be built the same ceremony must be gone through and the birds must be heard on the left. Before a war expedition they must be heard on the right.

When a house is almost finished the chief and his head-man go out early one morning to listen for the *nendak* on the left. If they hear it they light a fire, which must be kept burning; the chief stays by it while his aide-de-camp goes back to tell the people to pack up and bring their possessions. When they join the chief their goods are set down; after some betel-chewing they all go on, and when near the house they stop again. One of the men goes on to listen for the nendak, this time on the *right* side; he brings back a stick which he drives into the ground; on it he hangs a circlet of green creeper (the protector of his soul) and on this a hook, to prevent the soul from wandering. Such a stick, circlet and hook are set up for each family, with small pieces of bamboo for each member of it.

When they come to the house and take possession

of their rooms no one may go out after six o'clock. The medicine men pass their charms over every one to render them invisible to the evil spirits, and the framework of the house is covered with foliage lest spirits should rest on it. After this an old woman, carrying a basket, marches three times up and down the verandah simulating the action of paddy reaping. She then empties on to the fire the imaginary contents of her empty basket, the mosquitoes she has been reaping. Before the verandah may be used as a court of justice a ceremony called *mandi rumah* takes place. A sacrifice is made, a new ladder as entrance raised up, and then offerings are made to Pulang Gaya. One of the posts is struck with a bamboo holding rice, and the gods are implored to send down the seed of the *engkuni* tree to be used as a charm.

If a man on his way to his paddy farm hears a *papau* he must at once turn back, if he hears a *mbuas* on his right he must not venture out for five days. The call of a *kutok* bodes evil and that of a *katupong* means so much harm that he must stay away from the farm for three days and even longer unless he hears a *beragai*.

Should a Dyak set out to visit a friend and on his way hear a bad omen-bird he will at once go back. If he is building a boat and an unlucky bird flies over it the boat is forsaken. Should he be

SUPERSTITIONS AND THEIR EFFECTS 81

carrying timber for his house and hear a *kutok*, a *bejampong* or a *mbuas* he must drop the wood and leave it for some days or altogether.

A house will be deserted because a *beragai* has flown over it, or an armadillo crawled into it, or if an owl is heard making a particular noise; after the last, however, it is possible to return when some weeks have been passed in rough shelters, provided the *mbuas* and the *beragai* have been heard on the left.

Should a *katupong* fly through a house from end to end all the inhabitants must leave instantly, and huge demons will be seen and heard at night in possession.

In one district three birds are consulted during the day and two others at night; if one of the day-birds, the *keriak*, is heard on the right in an expedition it is well, if on the left success is doubtful; if its voice is in front danger lies ahead, and if behind the hearer must return at once, for serious evil threatens his home.

If an omen-bird is killed illness or death is sure to follow, unless the killing was accidental and a sacrifice is offered, but if a dead beast be found on a farm terrible consequences will ensue. A pig is killed and auguries deduced from the state of the body; if these are unfavourable the whole of the rice crop must be sold, for it is poisoned, and if the owner's family touch it some of them will die within the year, though strangers may eat it with impunity.

The burden of these omens comes into every part of the daily life, and can never be got away from. Certain men are supposed to have the gift of overcoming evil omens, and if they eat something off the farm they, through that, take away the curse. A piece of gold buried on the land, or the sacrifice of a fowl, buried, too, on the land, and its blood allowed to drop into a hole prepared for it, may neutralise the warnings of evil birds, but the result is very doubtful and so the haunting terrorism remains.

Disputes are often decided by an ordeal, generally that of diving, the man who can remain longest under water winning.

The night before the ordeal is to take place each party brings out, before witnesses, on to the verandah of his house, a certain amount of property as the stakes to go to his opponent if he wins the contest. Early the next morning this property is carried down to the river; the friends of each man assemble and get ready a fire by which to resuscitate their almost drowned champion. Two gratings are sunk in the river a few yards apart for the men to stand on, and a pole is given to each. Holding on to these poles, in water reaching to their waists, they plunge their heads under water at the same moment.

OFFERINGS TO OMEN BIRDS.

JUNGLE PATH.

All the people repeat wildly the word *lobön lobön*, their vigour and excitement increasing as either man shows sign of defeat. Anxious for the success of their own side some will hold down the head of their man under water if he seems to be giving in. So the contest goes on, a sickening spectacle, until one or other drops down and sinks below the water; then he is promptly rescued, carried off to the fire, and his face plastered over with mud by way of helping him to recover. Meanwhile the stakes have been triumphantly carried off by the victor's party.

Charms are greatly treasured; they may consist of an extraordinarily heterogeneous collection of things such as twigs, beads, small bones, deers' horns, Indian stones, bits of coral, but they are handed down for generations and their loss is believed to portend the extinction of the tribe. They are used for many purposes, from exorcising the evil *antu* which is causing a sickness, to enlisting the spirit of a mountain on behalf of travellers. Mountain-tops are supposed to be specially haunted by evil as well as good spirits, and trees, which nothing will induce the ordinary native to cut down, are left for their shelter. They look on with horror at Christian natives who venture to fell these groves and are much surprised when no evil happens to them.

A curious superstitious value is set upon the

sacred jars owned by the Dyaks. They are probably of Chinese manufacture, brought to Borneo nobody knows when. They are of coarse brown, glazed ware, and no tribe will part with them to strangers. The most valuable kind is the Gusi, green in colour, and about eighteen inches high; one of these is valued at £400. If a tribe by exchange or purchase can add to its stock a new jar it is received with a sacrifice, a chicken is waved over it to invoke a blessing, then the bird is killed and some of the blood sprinkled on the jar.

So daily, hourly, does this burden of superstitious observance press into the native life. We who stand in the liberty wherewith Christ has made us free, can in no wise picture the life of perpetual dread which such a system brings and which the Gospel light alone can dispel. And yet in this vivid realisation of the supernatural we have something to which we can appeal and on which to build.

QUESTIONS ON CHAPTER IV

1. Has the Dyak any sense of the supernatural?
2. What is the main idea beneath all their beliefs and superstitions?
3. Has the Dyak any conception of sin, any idea of moral improvement affecting his character?
4. What is the belief of the Land-Dyaks?
5. What do they think happens after death?

SUPERSTITIONS AND THEIR EFFECTS

6. Do they recognise any need for prayer?

7. Is the belief of the Land- and Sea-Dyaks the same?

8. Who are the *antus*, and what place do they hold in the people's lives?

9. In what way is the Dyaks' daily life affected by superstition?

10. How do they try to ward off the evils threatened by bad omens?

11. Does all this suggest any responsibility resting on ourselves?

CHAPTER V

History

IN the seventh century the Emperor of China would seem to have been overlord of at least part of Borneo, for there are records of tribute paid by Phala, on the north-east of the island, to China.

Two centuries later there was a considerable Chinese colonisation, probably chiefly in Brunei, where the people still show traces of Chinese ancestry. In 1575 there was again a large immigration from China, and through the latter part of the sixteenth, and on through the seventeenth century, a flourishing trade, especially in edible birds'-nests and certain woods, was carried on between the two countries.

Yet once again in the eighteenth century China sent over colonists, and the Malay princes, who ruled a great part of Borneo, invited them into their states, but would not allow them to enter into any commerce or agriculture, nor to possess arms or gunpowder.

In Europe the sixteenth century was the age of

Portugal and Spain. East and West their navigators were exploring and discovering new lands, and Borneo, hitherto known only to Eastern races, was reached either by Lorenzo da Gomez in 1518, or by Don Jorge da Menoza in 1526. Thus Portugal through the enterprise of her sons established a footing and commenced trade relations, and later on Spain coveted a share of the riches and tried to compete; but the day of both these countries was waning, and the next century was to belong to other nations. England was beginning her era of expansion. The East India Company's Charter for a monopoly of all English trade with the East Indies dated from 1600, and before long the Company had made settlements in Borneo as well as in other islands of the Malay Archipelago. But Britain was not yet mistress of the seas. Dutch fleets were pressing into every port, and on through the eighteenth century they almost monopolised the trade in cinnamon, nutmegs, cloves and spice, and were paramount on the western and southern coasts of Borneo.

In the north, England had kept a few factories, and in 1756 Alexander Dalrymple obtained from the Sultan of Sulu a grant of the island of Balambangan and all the north-east promontory of Borneo. A military post was established, but the natives destroyed it in 1775. By the end of the century the

English had entirely withdrawn, and in 1809 the Dutch, too, abandoned their settlements. Their occupation, though so extensive, had not led to the establishment of any rule or order, the country became a prey to native pirates, and trade was ruined. So serious was the condition that in 1811 the Sultan of Banjermassin sent an embassy to the English governor in Java asking him to take some steps to stop the raids. Alexander Hare was sent as Resident; he concluded a treaty with the Sultan, and received a grant of land which he colonised. Some years later this grant was cancelled and a free field left to the Dutch, who returned to the lands they had formerly held. Their policy soon reduced the country again to anarchy and confusion, and made it impossible for trade from Borneo to be carried on. Unchecked by any government, the Malay and Dyak pirates became a menace to English ships throughout the whole Archipelago.

At this time a young Englishman passed through these seas, and the spirit of adventure fired him with the wish to explore the islands, so beautiful and so full of mystery. James Brooke was born in 1803; he entered the East India Company's service, and was severely wounded in a war with Burmah. Invalided home he was granted a life pension of £70 a year, and for nearly five years was pronounced unfit to return to India. At last he sailed, but first

SIR JAMES BROOKE,
First Rajah of Sarawak.
(*From a Portrait in the "Illustrated London News," Nov., 1847.*)

a shipwreck and then a voyage in a very slow vessel delayed his arrival until the limit of his leave had expired. When he landed he was told that being overdue his billet had been given to another. Perhaps he was not over-anxious to plead the reasonable excuses which, with his father's interest, might have availed; the glamour of the sea and of a life of greater excitement had seized him, and taking for granted that the decision was irrevocable and that he was too late to be received back by the Company, he sailed on in the same vessel to China. He returned to England, and on his father's death inherited a fortune of £30,000 which enabled him to carry out his wish. He bought a yacht, and after proving her seaworthiness by cruises in the Mediterranean, he sailed in 1838 for Singapore. When he arrived there a tale of good treatment received from Muda Hassim, the Rajah of Sarawak, had just been brought by a shipwrecked crew, and Mr. Brooke was asked to take presents and letters of thanks in acknowledgment. So was he led, as men would say "by accident," to his life's work. A shipwreck, a native's kindness, the coincidence that the news should come as Brooke reached Singapore, were the threads by which God worked out His purpose.

All the islands were unknown lands to the Englishman, and he was as ready to go to Borneo as to any other; he set out, sailed up the Sarawak River and anchored off Kuching on 15th August, 1839. The country was nominally under the rule of the Sultan of Brunei, but his uncle, Muda Hassim, had been sent to this province to put down a rebellion, and held the position of Rajah. Brooke was kindly received and obtained permission for English trading ships to come. After staying for some time he sailed to visit other places, but came back the following year. Muda Hassim's weak policy had quite failed to restore peace; for four years war had been going on between the Malay rulers and the Dyaks; the Rajah was weary of it and offered to hand the country over to Brooke; this offer he declined unless it should be renewed at the end of a year, but he joined Bedrudeen, Muda Hassim's brother, in the hills, and their joint energy brought the war at last to a close. The next year the Rajah was still of the same mind, and on 24th September, 1841, he made over the government of Sarawak and its dependencies to James Brooke; this cession was formally confirmed in the following year by the Sultan of Brunei, the conditions being that a small annual payment should be made to the Sultan of Brunei, and that the laws and religion of the country should be respected. Thus arose one of the most picturesque incidents of history, when a Mohammedan ruler, whose race had for centuries governed a native state,

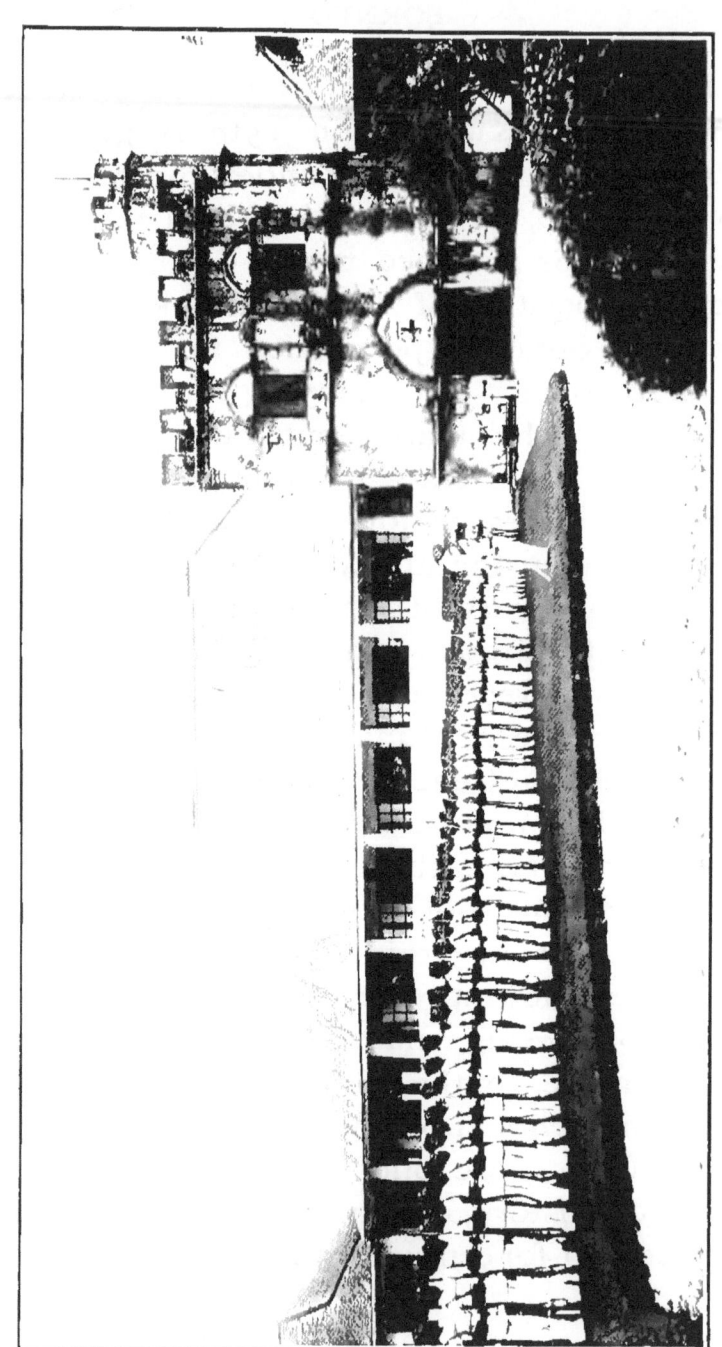

The Astana.
(The Rajah's Palace.)

voluntarily placed himself and his subjects in the hands of a young Englishman.

Seldom has a trust been accepted with higher aim or from more disinterested motives. Brooke's ambition was not to act for himself, but to show how an English gentleman was bound to act. He had studied the Malay character, had seen their innate cunning, deceit and intrigue, and he set himself to show them something better, to step in between the corrupt rulers and the oppressed tribes, with ideas of justice which they had never known, and the conception of which was entirely beyond their comprehension.

For one man, a solitary representative of Western civilisation, to attempt to introduce law and order, protection of property, and respect for human life, to give to people who for centuries had been robbed and down-trodden a sense of security, and, harder still, to restrain those who had lived and grown strong by a career of pillage and of plunder, must have seemed beyond human power. But, undertaken and carried out as it was in a spirit free from all personal ambition, seeking solely the welfare of the peoples, cruel on the one hand, crushed on the other, committed to his charge, absolutely without thought of individual gain, there was surely Divine guidance vouchsafed to this young ruler, which enabled him to bring his country into peace and safety. Practical common-sense and English straight-dealing won the day. When certain tribes raided a weak one in his territory and carried off the wives and children, Brooke sent letters to their three "sheriffs," stating that he wished to be on good terms with them, but that if any Dyaks "rob people in my country" it would be necessary for him to attack the place from whence they came.

The Chinese settlements brought difficulties too. There is an amusing account of one. A *kunsi* or company had been granted by Muda Hassim the right of working gold on a certain part of the river. The agreement was in Malay, and a Chinese translation had been made. Rajah Brooke discovered that this translation gave the *kunsi* an exclusive right to work gold and antimony over the whole country. He called them up, and explained how such a perversion would, from its deceit, which he hoped had been unintentional, make their name fall very low. He told them that a new *kunsi*, Simbok, would settle on the other branch of the river. Against this they protested, offering to receive any number into their own *kunsi*. The Rajah told them that any claims they might have had had been invalidated by their deceit, and they returned to consider the position. The next night they came, prepared to agree to the Simbok coming if they might be called Sam Simbok (slaves). To

HISTORY 93

Brooke's refusal they argued that their name San Ti Qu had three syllables, and it was better the others should have three syllables also. The Rajah said he would be delighted to agree to any terms denoting their equality, and as it was a pity they should not have the honour of the longer name he would agree to Sam Simbok provided they became Sam San Ti Qu. Of course they refused, so the war schooner and prahus were got ready, but the next night they came back, agreeing to accept the new company peaceably without the obnoxious 'Sam' syllable.

The Rajah formed a council, on which from the first he associated with himself the former rulers, the Malay Datus, so that they were consulted on all important steps. Eight natives were on this council, and finding it necessary to have some Europeans to help in developing the country, some young men were brought out from England, of whom four were brought into the council. In later years these numbers have been altered, and on the Supreme Council now are the Rajah, two Europeans and four Malays approved by the Rajah, and a general council of fifty members meets once in three years. In eight months the country became fairly peaceful; open courts for justice, presided over by the Rajah, were established, before which both civil and criminal cases were brought, and all exaction and extortion were stopped. The poor

Hill-Dyaks, who, helpless in the hands of the Malays, had been obliged to give up to them all they possessed, even wives and children, could now, for the first time, look forward to reaping what they had sown.

So for some years the little band of Englishmen worked on, but no civilisation has ever changed the moral nature of a people, and Rajah Brooke saw that his people needed more than he could give them.

"I am very decided on the great advantage to the commerce of the Archipelago by the development of this place, and more decided still on the vast field for Christianity. In a native state the missionary does not succeed because his efforts are counteracted by the contempt and the violence of Malay rulers, and the oppression practised on the Dyak tribes renders them averse to all instruction which flows from the Malays, or through them, and it is quite out of the power of the poor missionary to bring them relief or happiness. Here, however, this power would be his; he would be their guardian angel, he would be the local authority to encourage them. He would have every advantage, and his doctrine would be beneficially introduced by the amelioration of the temporal condition of a most unhappy race. I should expect a rapid advance in Christianity when once they were relieved from oppression." So wrote Sir James Brooke in his journal.

He did his part in "relieving them from oppression"; little could he have expected that the Church at home would be deaf to the call, blind to the opening for a "rapid advance," that the work all along would be so hampered by lack of men that the waiting fields could not be occupied, and, worse still, that, as years went on, fields which *had* been tilled, souls which *had* been won for Christ, should be left a prey for the enemy, the wheat choked by tares.

Though comparative peace reigned in the country, pirates continued to raid the coasts, harassing merchant vessels, and carrying on a slave trade. Determined to put this down, Sir James Brooke obtained the assistance of some English men-of-war under Captain Keppel's command, and gave the raiders of Sarebas and Skarang a severe lesson. Some years later unfair reports of this action were made in Parliament, representing that the people punished were not pirates and impeaching the Rajah's motives. The agitation dragged on, and twice, in 1850 and again in 1851, Mr. Hume asked for a Royal Commission to be appointed to inquire into the circumstances; on each occasion it was refused by majorities increasing from 105 to 218, only 18 members voting for the motion in 1851. On this occasion Lord Palmerston appealed to the House to negative the motion and so proclaim to the world that Sir James Brooke "retires from the investigation with an untarnished character and with unblemished honour". And, he added, " I am persuaded that he will continue to enjoy the esteem of his countrymen as a man who, by braving difficulties, by facing dangers in distant climates and in previously unknown lands, has done much to promote the commercial interests of his country, and to diffuse the light of civilisation in regions which have been before in the darkness of barbarism ".

Lord Aberdeen's ministry came in on 1st January, 1853. On 15th March Lord John Russell said in the House that they had no intention of instituting an inquiry previous to Sir James Brooke's departure from England. What then was the Rajah's surprise on the 30th March, the eve of his sailing, to receive a letter from Lord Wodehouse stating that the Government considered it expedient that an inquiry should be instituted into his position in the island and his relations with the native chiefs. Deeply pained, he had only time for one interview with Lord Clarendon. He reached Singapore on 24th May, and was soon carried across to Sarawak. Even before he landed he was seen to be ill, and as soon as he knew that he had small-pox he sent nearly every one away. His nephew, Captain Brooke, who had governed during the Rajah's absence, remained with him as well as Mr. Crookshank. Bishop McDougall was in England and no

SEA-DYAK WOMAN.

other doctor at hand; the Rajah, however, pulled through, to face a long and trying suspense before the commission, which at last issued, sat at Singapore. After still longer delay the Government report was received, entirely exonerating Sir James Brooke, and Lord Clarendon wrote that the Government were anxious that "he should be enabled to pursue the good work he had already so successfully carried on". During these years he had been quietly putting down piracy and head-hunting. He had built forts at various points, in each of which he placed a young Englishman as Resident to enforce order. At the commission one witness had said: "The distinction between the two kinds of Dyaks is this—the inland Dyaks take heads on shore, while the Sarebas and Skerang take them both on shore and sea". In one house this witness had found fifty or sixty heads and feared his own might go as an additional ornament; he had offered seventy or eighty rupees for one head, which was refused. The natives were led to understand clearly that the fines enforced for breaking the law did not go into the Rajah's pocket, but were used for improvements in the country; they were exacted because the Rajah had said that piracy was to be abolished, and abolished it should be.

Just after the cloud of worry about the commission had lifted a new trial came. A Chinese company working gold some distance above Kuching had been allowed a considerable measure of local government; when, however, its consumption of opium dropped suspiciously by one-half, there was no doubt that extensive smuggling was going on, and the *kunsi* was ordered to pay for as much opium as they had formerly used; they objected, and demonstrated their objection by descending without warning on the town. On the night of 18th February, 1857, yells and shrieks were heard; the Chinese rushed to the Rajah's house, set fire to that and other houses and killed one Englishman. Another Englishman and two English children were killed, and a Government official and his wife terribly wounded. The attack was so sudden that at first Sir James Brooke, who was ill, thought all was lost, and fled to Quab, one of the out-stations. When the news spread hundreds of faithful Malays and Dyaks flocked in, and when a small steamer arrived the Rajah was able to re-take the town. The Chinese were pursued and driven out by the angry natives and peace was soon restored. Among the Dyaks who helped most in the affair were the Skerangs who, but a short time before, had been punished for their lawlessness. Thus was the wisdom of a just rule vindicated.

Two years later a Malay plot was discovered, instigated by a Datu, to whom, since none of his

HISTORY 99

own relatives would be responsible for his conduct, the Rajah had been obliged to suggest an enforced absence from Sarawak after he had been convicted of treason. In this rising two Englishmen in an isolated fort were killed. Both the Rajah and his vice-gerent, Captain Brooke, were in England, but Mr. Johnson, the present Rajah, by strong measures averted greater peril at the time. The Malays, the Chinese and the Dyaks had thus impartially felt the strength of the white hand, and had learnt that the benefits of settled government and secure trade involved submission to the authority which brought them those good things. But a dark time came. The fact of the commission and the refusal of the English Government to grant any sort of protectorate had injured the Rajah's prestige, a thing so important with native races; he had spent thousands of his own money on the country, and was now in grave financial difficulties; a company, to which all the minerals except gold had been leased on payment of certain royalties, was in embarrassment, which, though fortunately it proved to be only temporary, was serious at the time; a Mohammedan impostor had raised unrest, and some of the tribes were getting out of hand. The Rajah, in failing health though he was, undertook the journey out again in order to strengthen Captain Brooke's hands, and, as he writes in a letter home, accomplished the work he went to do: (1) Peace with Brunei; (2) the bloodless conquest of Muka; (3) addition of all districts in dispute to the rule of Sarawak.

As the Sultan saw the benefits accruing to the English-governed portion of the country he had from time to time handed over more and more territory to the Rajah's rule, to become a trust in our charge, and as we have seen commerce was extended and peace increased.

Differences of opinion between the Rajah and Captain Brooke, whom he had meant to succeed him, caused him to change his arrangements, and on his death in 1868 he was succeeded by another nephew, Sir Charles Brooke, G.C.M.G., under whom the prosperity of Sarawak has become more and more settled. In 1864 the state had been so far recognised that the English Government accredited to it a consul, but the Rajah was not permitted to see in his lifetime what he had so earnestly wished for, his beloved country received as a Protectorate of the British Crown. This took place in 1889.

The northern part of the island came to us later. An English trading company received a Royal Charter to occupy the territory of North Borneo in 1880, and in 1888 it was declared a Protectorate of Great Britain. Two years later, Labuan, which since 1847 had been a Crown Colony, was placed under the administration of this Chartered Company,

Bassano.

Sir Charles Brooke, G.C.M.G.,
Rajah of Sarawak. Succeeded 1868.

and in 1898 the Sultan of Brunei transferred to them certain further districts, for which they pay a subsidy to him and his chiefs.

Practically, therefore, the whole of North Borneo (except the little wedge of Brunei) down to Cape Datu is under English influence. It has been brought to us in a wonderful way, first by the "accidental" landing of an adventurous Englishman, whose personality was just such as to win the confidence of the inhabitants, and then, owing to his wise government, other districts of the country were entrusted to him. The romantic story of the English Rajah drew attention to Borneo, and trading companies were glad to avail themselves of the security his rule afforded them. So the knowledge of the wealth of the island spread, and brought other traders in to develop this northern part.

Not without purpose in the counsels of God surely has all this been brought about, and such a land been given to us.

The story of Sarawak is unique. All through the well-being of the country has been the sole aim of its rulers; no thought of personal gain, no wish for self-aggrandisement has conflicted with what they saw was best for the people. Plunder and bloodshed have been put down, but not in order that the labour of a peaceful people might be exploited for the enrichment of the Government. By the cessation of wars and by the attraction of the Chinese and Indian labourers, the population has been vastly increased. Kuching, in 1844 a small Malay village with some forty wretched Chinese shops, is now a well-planned town of 15,000 inhabitants.

Year by year, as trade reaches further inland the country becomes more civilised, and through intercourse of Europeans with the natives their superstitions and beliefs will die out; their minds will be left as it were swept and garnished, emptied of the old ideas of worship which, though full of error, still brought them some feeling of a Power greater than themselves. In civilisation they see the white man's sense of justice, of honour, of mercy. A dim sense of something higher than they have known steals over them. Whence does the white men get these qualities? Are they for them too to learn?

A thousand years ago the ancestors of those same white men were perhaps as wild and lawless as they. What brought for him the change? It was the gift then of the East to the West; the gift of the apostolic preaching of Christ crucified reaching on through Corinth and Ephesus, and Rome, to the isles of the sea; so were the Picts and the Britons converted to Christianity and taught of the Resurrection strength in which they might conquer the powers of darkness. Now it must be the gift of the West to the East. Fifteen centuries of Christian-

PADAS RIVER.
(British North Borneo.)

ity have at least left their mark on our nation, but the poor savage cannot win through civilisation alone. He must learn of God's love, he must feel that God wants him, he must awaken to the fact of sin, must realise his need of forgiveness and must be taught that only by the strength of the Holy Spirit in him can he come out from the bondage in which he has been born.

QUESTIONS ON CHAPTER V

1. What was the earliest known connection between Borneo and China?

2. In what way did Europe first come into contact with Borneo? Relate the early dealing with English people.

3. What do you know of the history of Rajah Brooke? How did he become concerned with Sarawak?

4. When and why was the Government handed over to him, and by whom?

5. What principles always inspired Rajah Brooke in his government of Sarawak?

6. What success did he meet with, and whence came his greatest hindrances?

7. Was there any dissatisfaction at home, how was it expressed, and was it found to be substantiated?

8. Did the natives themselves appreciate the justice of his rule?

9. What is the present relationship between England and Borneo?

10. What did Rajah Brooke feel was needed besides the blessing of good and impartial government.

CHAPTER VI

Sixty Years of Missions

WE have seen that in 1839, Sir James Brooke first landed in Sarawak. His rule, wise and strong, did very much for the country, but, as his diary tells, he felt that a higher teaching than that of civil rule alone was needed, and, during a visit to England in 1847 he appealed to the church at home to help him in establishing a mission. Neither the S.P.G. nor C.M.S. saw their way to undertake the work, so a personal friend of the Rajah's, the Rev. A. D. Brereton, organised a committee, of which the Earl of Ellesmere was President, Admiral Sir H. Keppel, Admiral C. D. Bethune, Canon Rylewood, and Mr. Brereton were the other members, with the Rev. I. F. Stooks as Hon. Secretary. Their object was to collect and administer funds to support a mission in Sarawak under the Rajah's protection, with the hope of spreading Christianity throughout the island of Borneo, and the adjacent

Francis Thomas (McDougall),
D.C.L.,
Bishop of Labuan and Sarawak,
1855-1868.

Mrs. McDougall.

countries. Funds soon came in, the Queen Dowager headed the list and S.P.G. gave £50 a year.

In June, 1847, the Archbishop of Canterbury and the Bishop of London appointed the Rev. F. McDougall of Magdalen Hall, Oxford, a fellow of the Royal College of Surgeons, as head of the mission. The Rev. W. Wright, and the Rev. S. Montgomery were chosen to work with him. Mr. Montgomery died of fever caught whilst visiting in his English parish, so only Mr. McDougall and Mr. Wright with their wives and children sailed for Borneo in November, 1847. They did not reach Kuching until June, 1848. They were warmly welcomed by the English residents, and by the Rajah's arrangement were housed in a large building erected by a German Missionary who had been recalled, and of which the lower part was now used as a court-house, In the rooms above, the two missionaries and their families lived for some months. In one small room Mr. McDougall opened a dispensary where he received patients for two or three hours each day: in this way he made friends with many of the people, and also learned a good deal of the Malay language. For part of the day this same room was used as a school for a few adults who wanted to learn more English.

As soon as he arrived, Mr. McDougall had decided on the ground he would *like* for the church and mission house, and when the Rajah, who was absent for a time, came back, he generously made a grant of forty acres of land for mission purposes. This land contained two small hills, one of which was to be crowned by the church, the other by the mission house. The top of the second hill was cleared from jungle and soon levelled, Malays being employed for the work, as the Chinese who began it resolutely refused to give up the slow procedure of using their small baskets and hoes, instead of the wheelbarrows and shovels provided for them. The ground floor of the house was devoted to school work; a large schoolroom ran through the centre, with, on one side, the dormitories, and on the other the matron's and girls' rooms. Above the schoolroom was the McDougalls' dining room, on one side of it was their bedroom and library and on the other were rooms for missionaries. A third storey gave three rooms in the roof. The house was built of the hard bilian wood, and the roof was covered with shingles of the same. Later another house was built close by for a boys' school. The mission house was finished in about a year, and the McDougalls were thankful to move into it from their abode beneath which the river ran: they were now alone, for before this Mr. Wright had given up the work and gone to Singapore.

The next work, the church, was now to be begun.

As Mr. McDougall wrote, he had to be not only architect, but head joiner, carpenter and blacksmith, and had to make working models for everything; he and Mrs. McDougall prepared the plans, and on 28th August, 1850, the first "stone" was laid and the Rajah in full uniform as governor of Labuan, with a yellow umbrella held over him by a Malay, lowered the great block of wood into its place. The beams, rafters and posts were all squared and made ready in bilian wood like the house; the arches and mouldings were carefully finished in bilian, nibong and miraboo and highly polished inside, and the walls were lined with cedar planks. Some ornamental pillars of nibong palm were put up, but had to be replaced, for the white ants ate them through. The pulpit, lectern, reading desk and chairs, were carved in Singapore, and there too was made the east window, representing in the centre light the Sarawak cross, red and black on a golden ground. For the font a large clam shell was treated with acid till it became a beautiful pearly white, and mounted on an ebony pedestal. The bell was made from broken gongs, cast by a Javanese workman. "Gloria in Excelsis," reads on it, with the names of Sir James Brooke and Mr. McDougall on either side. The building was consecrated on 22nd January, 1851.

For more than two years Mr. McDougall had

been working quite alone. At Kuching he had superintended the building of the church and mission house, he had held English, Malay and Chinese services, continued his medical work, established a school into which he took at one time no fewer than thirty children from a large body of Dyak-Chinese who took refuge at Kuching from another Dyak-Chinese tribe. Besides this he had visited among the Dyak tribes, and seen where work should be begun, if ever workers came. The Chinese work was very successful, an educated Chinese who came to Kuching, was engaged as translator and interpreter, and soon this Sing Sang came as a learner himself and after some years was ordained: the Chinese congregation increased greatly and the sincerity of the converts was shown in one way at least, by their keeping Sunday as a day of worship, when all their heathen countrymen around were working. When Mr. Horsburgh, a missionary who had worked in China, came to help Mr. McDougall, he was astonished at the success of his work among the Chinese compared with what he had seen in their own country. This work, so varied in kind, must have been overwhelming for one man, single-handed, yet no one came until, in 1851, Bishop Wilson of Calcutta crossed to Sarawak to consecrate the church dedicated to St. Thomas, and brought with him Mr. Fox to take

ORCHID.

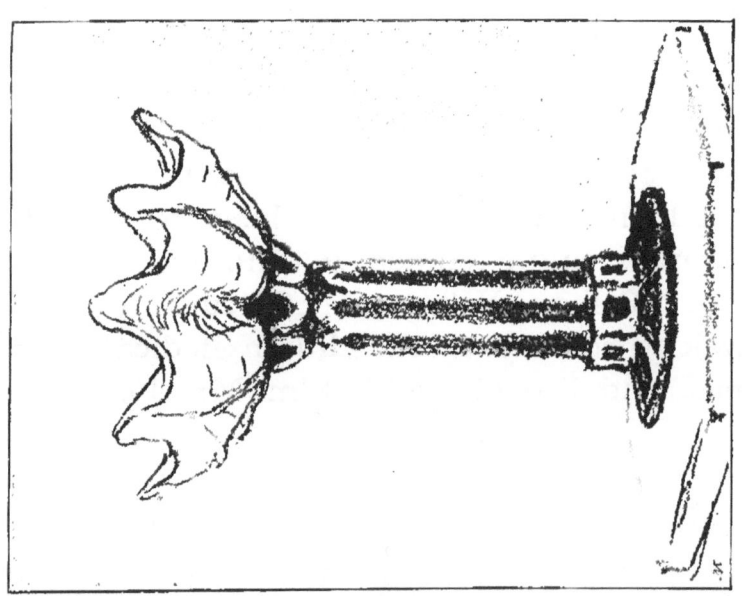

FONT.

charge of the native school. Mr. Nicholls, another student from Bishop's College, Calcutta, and the Rev. Walter Chambers came soon afterwards. In Bishop McDougall's memoirs he thus describes their life: "School begins at seven A.M.: we meet for church at eight: at nine o'clock we have breakfast: from ten o'clock to twelve o'clock I am employed with Fox and Nicholls at the Hospital and Dispensary, showing them practically what I can, and giving a daily lecture on the principles of medicine and surgery. Between noon and two P.M. I give them all three, Chambers included, a Malay lesson, and at three o'clock they take another lesson from a native till chapel time again at five o'clock, after which we walk or ride till seven o'clock and are all pretty well ready for bed at nine o'clock."

Mr. Nicholls did not stay long, and began the sad tale of the missionary roll of resignation and illness, illness not due necessarily to the climate, for some of the heroes of this outpost have laboured there for over thirty years.

At this time the funds of the Home Organisation failed; hearts had grown cold, and hands had grown weary. The Committee wrote that no more money was to be spent upon the Church, for which two outside aisles, to be used as Chinese and Malay schools, had been designed, and they refused to support the Chinese school: the children in it had all been baptised and were being regularly taught in the Faith; moreover, Mr. McDougall had promised to keep them for ten years: he asked, "How can I send my little Christians back to heathen homes when I have pledged myself to support them?" The Rajah and the Bishop of Calcutta both gave some help, and Mr. McDougall made himself responsible for the charge of eighteen of the children.

This crisis in affairs, his own illness, and a serious affection of the knee which failed to yield to any treatment obtainable within reach, and also the question of creating a bishopric for the Mission, made it advisable for the McDougalls to come to England in 1852. During their four years in Borneo they had lost three baby children as well as the little boy of two whom they took out, and the mother's heart must have yearned to see her one boy left in England, though she little thought how soon he too was to be taken from them. Before they arrived steps had been taken at home which resulted in the work of the Borneo Church Mission being handed over to S. P. G. From that time, until on his consecration in 1909, Dr. Mounsey established the "Borneo Mission Association in connection with S.P.G.," as a special fund, the whole cost of the Mission has been borne by the old society, except for one sum invested for the

St. Thomas', Kuching (Pro-Cathedral).

Episcopal Endowment, of which the interest provides £270 per annum towards the bishop's stipend.

The question of the bishopric was delayed by many technical difficulties, for it was then thought impossible to appoint a missionary Bishop outside the Dominion of the Crown. After long debate it was decided that the title might be taken from the only spot of land near Sarawak under the control of the Colonial Office, the island of Labuan. There was no doubt that Dr. McDougall should be chosen as the bishop, but still further delay arose in getting the commission for his consecration. At last he decided to return to Sarawak, and when the formalities were completed he went back to Calcutta, and there, on St. Luke's Day, 1855, took place the first consecration of an English bishop out of England. The Rajah declined to recognise in his territory any rights of a Bishop of Labuan, but this difficulty was got over by his giving Dr. McDougall jurisdiction as also Bishop of Sarawak.

There were now three clergy working there. Mr. Chalmers had been sent to open a mission to the Sea Dyaks at Banting, on the Lingga River, a tributary of the Batang Lupar. Mr. Horsburgh, suited for Chinese work, had been left in charge at Kuching during Dr. McDougall's absence in England: the climate however proved too trying and after three years he left. Mr. Gomes, from Ceylon, went to the natives of the Sibuyow and Balau tribes at Lundu, sixty miles west of Kuching. The Malay Mohammedan influence was strong there, but after two years and a half, eight converts were baptized, and in 1855, a church, the second in Sarawak territory, was opened.

In that year two students from Bishop's College, Calcutta, and a clergyman from England arrived: two of them soon left, Mr. Koch remained. Not for three years did any more recruits appear—then Mr. Chalmers, Mr. Glover and Mr. Hacket came. At the end of 1859, Dr. McDougall was ordered home, and in the following year these three clergy gave up the work, two of them on account of the climate went to Australia, and the third became alarmed for the safety of his wife and child in the Chinese and native outbreaks.

In 1861, four men were sent out from England, and in June of that year the Bishop ordained Mr. Crosland and Mr. Mesney (from St. Augustine's College) and Mr. Abé and Mr. Zehnder, deacons; of these Archdeacon Mesney worked there for thirty-six years and Mr. Zehnder for thirty-two.

In 1864, the Bishop called his clergy together in synod to discuss matters relating to the discipline and temporalities of the church, and questions of order and ritual in the native missions. This first synod began with a declaration that the church in Sarawak was an integral portion of the Anglican Church, and in his last charge, delivered in 1866, the Bishop said, " I feel persuaded that we can only maintain our position in this country by true unswerving allegiance to our English mother ; we are purely a missionary church, militant in a heathen and Mohammedan country—the church in Borneo, not the church of Borneo—wholly unable to stand alone, and dependent for its support upon the alms of the church at home administered by the S.P.G."

The two synods which followed, 1865 and 1866, were occupied with the important matter of settling how theological terms should be translated in the Malay, Land and Sea-Dyaks' languages. Two years after his arrival the Bishop had translated the catechism into Malay, and in 1857 had completed the Translation of the Prayer Book which was published by S.P.C.K. Years of fever and rheumatism had undermined his health, and after the last synod he was taken ill with heart trouble ; at the end of the year he had to return to England, and in the spring of 1868, finding there was little chance of his being able again to live in Sarawak, he resigned.

Bishop McDougall had laid firm and wise foundations of episcopal and missionary work. As one of his successors wrote, " In his selection of the chief centres of operation, a great matter in a new country, he made no mistakes. We are occupying them still and in no case regret the selection, though the operations of the mission have naturally extended much further since his departure, and in all our work we are going on in the old lines which he laid down, sometimes getting back to them after they had been abandoned for a while. In fact, as I have often said, we are reaping in these days the harvest which was sown at the beginning of the mission, and the present generation thankfully acknowledges the debt they owe to the pioneer Bishop and his fellow workers."

Mrs. McDougall had been a true help-meet to her husband. From the first much of the care of the Chinese school devolved on her: catering for the big household, teaching the children to sing, having them often with her in their walks and play-time, and, when the great influx of Chinese children came, helping to provide clothes for them ; we have seen too how her talent for drawing was requisitioned in preparing sketches and plans for the building of the church.

When the Chinese insurrection came in 1857, Mrs. McDougall went through terrible experiences. After they had spent two nights of awful suspense in Kuching where the rebel Chinese miners were burn-

A Family of Christian Dyaks.

ing and pillaging houses, and killing the English, men, women and children, the Bishop insisted that she and her three children, with Miss Woolley, a lady who had gone out to work in the mission, should go on board a vessel for Singapore. Any woman would a thousand times rather have stayed by her husband in danger, but with true courage she consented, knowing that it would lesson his anxiety to feel that they were in safety. In a night of pitch darkness and heavy rain they were rowed down the river in a boat crammed full of Chinese women, children and boxes. When they reached the schooner waiting at the mouth of the Sarawak, and climbed on board, they found the only cabin occupied by Chinese, and that there was no place for them but the open deck. Mrs. McDougall could not expose her children to the wet all night, so there was nothing but to get back into the boat. One faithful man was with them, but the boat was too heavy for him to move alone. As they were stranded, cold, wet and miserable in mid-stream, the face of an English friend appeared in the darkness in a boat alongside theirs. With his crew he rowed them up to some Malay houses where he and the boy slept, while Miss Woolley and the two little girls lay down on the thwarts of the boat, and Mrs. McDougall sat in the bottom to watch lest the children fell off. We can well believe she had no inclination to go to sleep.

In the morning they were taken in and hospitably cared for by the Malays. In the evening a message from the Bishop said he thought they might safely return to Kuching. Joyfully the little party of women and children set out, but on their way smoke was seen rising above the trees. What did it mean? Boats with fugitives met them; an Englishwoman, who had been left for dead the first night, then rescued and taken to the McDougalls' house, children, English and Chinese, and one of the Missionaries were coming away. From them they learnt that the rebels, furious at the Bishop's support of the Rajah, had tried to kill him, and had then again set fire to and ransacked the town. Again the little party had to return to their Malay quarters and to wait anxious hours till the Bishop joined them. After that they all went to the fort at Lingga, some distance up the Batang Lupar River, where they were in safety, but there was little food, and some of the children became so ill that a move had to be made to some place where they could get more than rice and gourds.

Mr. Chambers received them at Banting, and they stayed there safely until it was possible to return to Kuching. It was at Banting that the gruesome feast happened which Mrs. McDougall describes so graphically. "One day we were invited to a feast in one of the long houses. I said, 'I hope we shall see no heads,' and was told I need not see any; so taking Mab in my hand I went with Mr. Chambers and we climbed up into the long verandah room where all the work goes on. This long house was surrounded with fruit trees and very comfortable. There were plenty of pigs under the house, and fowls perching in every direction. About thirty families lived in the house; the married people having each their little room to themselves, and the long room I spoke of, being used for cooking, mat-making, paddy-beating, and all the usual occupations of their lives. We were seated on white mats and welcomed by the chief people present. The feast was laid on a raised platform along the side of the room. There were a good many ornaments of the betel-nut palm plaited into ingenious shapes standing about the table so that I did not at first remark anything else. As we English folks could not eat fowls roasted in their feathers, nor cakes fried in cocoa-nut oil, they brought us fine joints of bamboo filled with pulut rice, which turns to a jelly in cooking, and is fragrant with the scent of the young cane. I was just going to eat this delicacy when my eyes fell upon three human heads standing on a large dish, freshly killed, and slightly smoked, with food and sirih leaves in their mouths. Had I known them when alive I must have recognised them for they looked quite natural. I looked with alarm at

Mab, lest she should see them too, then we made our retreat as soon as possible. But I dared say nothing. These Dyaks had killed our enemies and were only following their own customs by rejoicing over their dead victims. But the fact seemed to part them from us by centuries of feeling—our disgust and their complacency. . . . This was my first and last visit to a Dyak feast".

When Bishop McDougall resigned, Archdeacon Chambers was at once chosen as his successor, and consecrated in 1869; the Straits Settlement being afterwards added to the Diocese. Since 1851 this devoted missionary had been working most zealously at Banting; he had mastered the Sea-Dyak language and reduced it to writing. A substantial church had been consecrated in 1859, and here and at Lundu many Dyaks had been baptised, and six became catechists. But Mr Chambers' influence had reached much further than his own district. One Dyak staying for a time in Banting came for instruction and was baptised; he became head of his village far inland, and for ten years, entirely alone, he taught his people, gathering them together regularly for prayer in the church which they built. Another, the son of a pirate, was also taught and baptised; some months afterwards he brought his wife and daughter for instruction, and when, four years later, Mr. Chambers visited his tribe, he found,

WALTER (CHAMBERS), D.D.,
Bishop of Labuan and Sarawak,
1869-1880.

GEORGE FREDERICK (HOSE), D.D.,
Bishop of Singapore, Labuan and
Sarawak, 1881-1908.

after thorough examination, that no fewer than 180 of them had been so carefully taught that he had no hesitation in baptising them at once. At the time of his consecration there were about 1,000 Dyaks and 200 Chinese Christians, and four churches and three chapels had been built. It had been impossible even to attempt work in the interior or in North Borneo, and Labuan had only very occasional visits from the Bishop.

Bishop Chambers carried on the work with the same devotion which he had shown at Banting, but without more clergy great progress could not be made. In 1879 he was obliged to resign, and returned to England paralysed, to end his days, the wreck of a strong man.

He was succeeded by Dr. Hose, who had been Colonial Chaplain to the Straits and was consecrated as Bishop of Singapore, Labuan and Sarawak in the chapel at Lambeth Palace on Ascension Day, 1881. In the first seven years of his Episcopate he confirmed over 1,000 people and there were 1,700 baptisms: the number of native Christians rose to 3,800, and since that has increased to 6,000. The Dyaks proved their earnestness by building at least 18 little prayer-houses at their own cost, where native catechists taught them what they could. One day a Dyak from the Saribas, one of the parts from which pirates once came, begged Archdeacon

Sharp at Kuching to ask for a " Surah Sambeyang," Prayer Book, meaning one on religion: to the Archdeacon's surprise he found that he wanted one of the Gospels and that he could read it. The touching explanation was brought out that some years ago, a boy from their tribe who was taught at the Kuching school, had gone home. "And when he told us about God and the Christian religion it seemed very good to us, and we made him teach us all he could. Next we asked him to teach us to read, and when some of us had learnt we taught the others. And now there are many of us in our country who believe in God and in Jesus Christ although no missionary lives amongst us." It was found that those people used to get books to take on their gutta-percha expeditions into the forests, and teach each other during the long evenings, and this is by no means an isolated instance.

One of the first claims upon Dr. Hose's attention after his arrival in Sarawak in January, 1882, was the necessity of providing a new and more commodious school. The raising of the funds for this purpose took some years; in 1886, however, a firm solid brick building was erected on the Mission ground. In it 250 boys are now being taught, of whom 70 are boarded in the house. Bishop McDougall's old school was then repaired and adapted to be the girls' school of the Mission, but the time

BANTING DYAKS.

has come for it to be replaced by a larger and better edifice. It is now in a most ruinous and unsatisfactory condition, overcrowded and insanitary.

Other new buildings in the years that followed were two houses for the printer, and for the Chinese catechist, the latter building being large enough to be used as a guest-house for Christian Chinese coming in from the country districts to worship.

A house was also built where Dyak visitors could be received and Dyak patients nursed; this was placed near the girls' school, so that its occupants might have the ministrations of 'Sister Mary' (Miss Sharp).

Lastly a large club was erected where old schoolboys residing in the town might meet, and both amuse and inform themselves, while keeping in touch with their old teachers.

This does not profess to be a complete history of the Mission. In such a work there would be much to tell of the labours of Mr. (afterwards Archdeacon) Mesney in Banting and at Kuching; how in Banting he sallied out into the forest with his faithful Dyaks, and selected and superintended the felling and bringing home of the great bilian trees which are the pillars of the great church there, and how strenuously he worked in all departments of the Mission till, after twenty-six years, failing health sent him home.

There would be much to say too of Mr. Perham's work among the Krian people and the Balaus for twenty years before he was selected for the larger work of Colonial Chaplain and Archdeacon of Singapore. And of Mr. Gomes at Lundu for fifteen years, and of Mr. Leggatt at Skerang and elsewhere.

But the burden of any such history would have to be the sad fact that the mission has always been under-manned. Men have gone out, stayed a few years, in some cases only a few months, and then have been disheartened and have left for other scenes, or for some other reason have had to go.

Yet the hopefulness of the enterprise is abundantly manifest. It is to be seen in the steady, the large increase in numbers of the members of the church, in their conspicuous steadfastness in the faith, and in their loyal and affectionate attachment to the few pastors who have stayed with them.

Bishop Hose was assisted in his long years of labour by a devoted wife, whose quiet and beautiful life was an example and help to many, and the remembrance of whose words and works will ever remain an inspiration to those who knew her.

We must be content with the bare mention of

LUJAI, UKIT, OF THE UPPER REJANG.

the work done by other women workers, who have done so much and done it so well.

In 1908, Bishop Hose resigned and it was decided to divide the huge Diocese, to make Singapore and the Straits Settlements a separate Diocese again, and to give Borneo a Bishop of its own, with the original title of the See, Labuan and Sarawak.

QUESTIONS ON CHAPTER VI

1. What were the first steps taken at home in response to the Rajah's appeal for a missionary?
2. How was missionary work begun in Borneo? Where was the first church built, and when?
3. Show the many-sided character of Dr. McDougall's work.
4. Home interest and zeal began to flag. When and how was the work affected by this diminution of interest?
5. What difficulties had to be overcome before a Bishop could be appointed?
6. When was the first synod held, and what memorable dec lration was made thereat by the Bishop?
7. Is there any testimony to the value of Bishop McDougall's work, to his far-reaching forethought, and his grasp of the situation and of the future needs?
8. Show how great was the difficulty of persuading the Dyak to give up his savage customs.
9. Mention some events which have happened since

Bishop McDougall's resignation. What Bishops succeeded him?

10. Is there any evidence that the natives value Christianity?

11. What has been the saddest feature of mission work in Borneo?

CHAPTER VII

Position of the Church in Borneo in 1909

THE fourth Bishop of Labuan and Sarawak, Dr. Mounsey, was consecrated in Lambeth Palace Chapel on the Feast of the Annunciation, 1909. He had been led by God's Providence through spheres of work specially adapted to prepare him for the work to which he was now called. After being ordained in England he had had seven years' experience of work in Australia, and then had lived among the savages of New Guinea. Brought back to England to further the home work for that diocese, he had gained valuable experience on the Standing Committee of S.P.G. and on the Bishop of London's Evangelistic Council, of which he had been Honorary Secretary—had not only gained, but given, from his own knowledge of mission work, and had become known and valued by those in authority, who now, with full confidence in his wisdom and devotion, called him to go forth to this forlorn outpost of the Church. What was the position in which he found it?

There were only two English clergy in the whole of

Borneo, Archdeacon Sharp at Kuching, and in British North Borneo, the Rev. W. H. Elton at Sandakan. The Rev. W. Howell, educated at St. Augustine's College, Canterbury, was at Sabu, on the Undop. The Rev. Chung Ah Luk, the first Chinaman baptised by Dr. McDougall, who had been tested by ten years' service as a lay-reader, and then ordained deacon in 1874 and priest in 1904, was at Quop, and a Chinese deacon, Fong Han Gong, at Kudat. There were also twenty-six native teachers and fifteen lay-readers.

The late Bishop, as we have seen, had been consecrated in 1881 with the title of Bishop of Singapore, Labuan and Sarawak, with jurisdiction over the Straits Settlements. For this utterly unwieldy diocese Singapore was the headquarters; the Bishop had to spend six months there and six in Borneo, an arrangement which added to the cares and difficulties of the enormous area, by cutting him off for half the year from any personal dealing with the problems which were sure to arise in the other part of the diocese from that in which he was then resident. Now that it was divided, and Singapore and the Straits were to be made into a separate diocese, the Bishop would make his centre of work at Kuching.

Here Archdeacon Sharp was responsible for all ministrations to the European residents. Daily

KAYAN GIRL WITH EAR-RINGS.

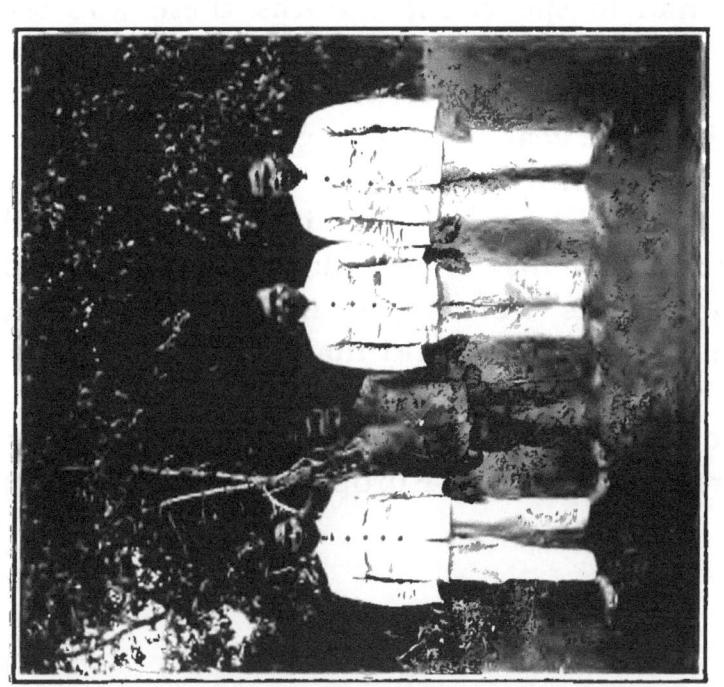
BOYS AT MERDANG SCHOOL.

services were held with a good choir of Dyaks and Chinese; these were in English, but services were also held in Chinese, Malay and Sea-Dyak. There was a boys' school where the boarders—Chinese, Eurasians, Land- and Sea-Dyaks—were all either Christians or receiving Christian instruction. The girls' school, under Miss Caroline Sharp, was hampered by the inadequacy of its buildings. It was absolutely necessary that a new school should be provided for the sixty pupils. There was the Dyak Rest-house, where, until she was obliged to come home ill, Miss Mary Sharp had nursed cases of slight illness, more serious cases being treated at the Government Hospital. A large Christian Dyak population had to be cared for; at the great festivals Sea-Dyaks came from great distances in their boats, sheltered by their palm-leaf awnings, to make their communion at the pro-Cathedral, and, literally, in the old words which we have sung and grown weary of because we did not realise their truth, "from many an ancient river, from many a palmy plain," these natives were continually coming to beg that teachers might be sent to them. At Merdang, twenty miles away up the Quop branch of the Sarawak River, there *had* been a congregation of a hundred people, but owing to Archdeacon Mesney's illness they had been left, and many had fallen back into heathenism.

Archdeacon Sharp took up this work again; two men of influence became mission workers, and the people built a substantial church. When this was completed they set to work on a school; ten boys were already sleeping in a loft belonging to Buda, the native catechist, and more wanted to come, so a schoolhouse was built, where the boys are taught industrial work as well as reading and writing; they have a poultry-farm and ground for planting paddy, pepper and vegetables, the sale of which helps to support the school.

Besides all this work and many other out-stations under Archdeacon Sharp's charge, there was a large Chinese population of planters and miners in and around Kuching, to be ministered to in four different dialects. Ten years before a hundred Chinese Hakkas, who had been converted in China, were brought in by the Sarawak Government to introduce new methods of rice planting. The Tiaochews and Foochows were asking to be taught, and for the large Hokien tribe only lately had even a catechist been found. A Chinese institute had just been built in the Mission grounds, where large numbers of Chinese were being brought into contact with their Christian teachers.

The Sebuyan Dyaks, on the Sarawak River, had been without a resident European missionary for years. Again and yet again petitions came from

Christ Church, Banting.

villages on more distant rivers for a teacher, and none could be sent. *How could the one man at Kuching do more?*

Banting had been the district of one of the worst head-hunting tribes; it was here that Bishop Chambers began his work with so great success: the number of converts increased largely, and several of them became evangelists to their own people. Archdeacon Perham had spent nineteen years in the jungle, working at Sebetan on the Krian River and at Banting. In his time there was an enthusiasm of religion at the latter place, and when he revisited Sarawak in 1907, after an absence of twenty years, he had received an extraordinarily warm welcome from his old friends on the Batang Lupar.

In 1904 the Rev. G. Dexter Allen had been appointed to Banting, with his wife, a qualified doctor. A boarding-school for boys was reopened and there were soon twenty scholars. Medical work had been begun, and in 1906 a small hospital was built. It is said that one doctor in the mission field creates work for at least one evangelistic missionary, and certainly here the medical work proved a means of winning the confidence of the people and brought up-river Dyaks to the Mission hill whom otherwise the padre would not have had the opportunity of teaching.

Here the church and mission houses stand on the top of a very steep hill; the path leads up by steps cut in the earth or rock, and in one place a ladder forty feet high against the face of a cliff must be mounted. Long ago the Dyaks used to live on the top of this hill for safety; they could see their enemies coming far away, and they beat gongs to warn their own people and to call them up the hill from the paddy fields below; then, if the enemy landed from their boats and tried to get up to them, they could throw them down, and their stronghold was never taken. Now that they are safe from fear of attack the houses are built near the river, but the church and the pretty parsonage still stand as a beacon in the old place.

This, the largest settlement of Sea-Dyaks in existence, was without a missionary in charge, as Mr. and Mrs. Dexter Allen were at home when the Bishop went out.

For want of men another station had had to be left in Mr. Allen's charge. That on the Krian River is three days' journey away from Banting, and it must be remembered that all these journeys have to be made in rowing boats. At Sebetan, once an important centre on this river, the church and mission lodge were in ruins, destroyed by white ants, because for so long there was no one to see to their care. One of the people when being asked about relapses into heathen practices said: "What can you expect after leaving us all these years without a shepherd. We do not want to lapse into the old ways, and if a padre will come and help us we will follow him. Is there no one in all your great country who will come and help us?"

It is easy to say that these people once taught should know better, but these Dyaks are one of the child-races of the world. The Chinese have had centuries of civilisation and of learning, which gives them a certain inherited stability of character, but a child-race needs to be led and guided step by step.

"Is there no one in all your great country who will come and help us?" say these children, and yet we pass by on the other side, and leave the wounded souls among thieves.

Lundu had been left for some time. Mr. Leggatt had to be called away when Mr. Elton went on furlough, and then he himself had to come home. His Dyaks, too, are not strong enough to be left, and there ought not to be the necessity. It was here that the first missionary offered to pay the Sebuyan tribe for a house they had built for him. They brought the money back, and one of the chief men, taking in his hand the translation of the Creed, the Lord's Prayer and the Ten Commandments, said: "This is worth more than any wages he can give us. Has anybody hitherto come to teach us the truths which now for the first time we are taught by him? Did not our former masters come to us only to plunder and tyrannise over us? Rather than look for remuneration we ought to be thankful that he comes to us at all, and to remember that the wish to have a house here is itself a proof of his affection for us."

The work in this district is consecrated by the labours during thirty-two years of Mr. Zehnder. Practically never having taken furlough, he was at last, by ill-health, compelled to resign in 1892, but his work and his life were to be given up together, and he did not live to see the steamer which was to have borne him home. Shall we let the fruits of his devotion pass away?

Sabu, on the Undop River, Skerang and Sarebas were under Mr. Howell. By incessant travelling and by opening little churches in villages where a few people had become Christians, and could bring others in, and also by means of two Rest-houses, where cases of illness were treated by him, and cared for, during his absence, by his wife, he had sown much seed, but as he wrote pathetically, " he could not do justice to his own district when he had to consider the claims of two others which were without European missionaries ". In Skerang, one of these, the people, as in other places, had fallen

DYAKS IN FULL DRESS.

CHRIST CHURCH, LUNDU.

away when they were left for years without a padre. The other, on the Sarebas, was one of the most promising places in Sarawak, but for *lack of a man* to take charge it had never become an independent mission. In the school at Sabu Mr. Howell could only take eighteen boys because *he had no funds for more*, and was obliged to close his ears to the applications from all sides that he would receive boys.

The Rev. Chung Ah Luk was in charge of Quop and its out-station. The Dyaks in this district are singularly musical, and without any organ take the whole choral service, singing in parts.

In British North Borneo, a district larger than Ireland, Mr. Elton was all alone. There was a governor and a considerable English population brought in by the British North Borneo Company, who needed the Church's ministrations, and who not only valued them for themselves, but helped liberally towards work among the heathen.

Mr. Elton's headquarters were at Sandakan, where, when there was no chaplain on board, he acted as such to the English and American warships which put in, and to the large number of merchant vessels visiting the port. By his exertions in raising funds and in training Chinese workmen, a beautiful stone church, the first in Borneo, had been built, and many settlers, Dutch and German, as well as English, living up the rivers, far away from the coast, looked to Mr. Elton for the only spiritual ministrations they could get.

Services for a considerable body of Chinese Christians here were held by a native catechist, partly supported by themselves. Malays, Chinese, Eurasians, Sulus, Muruts, and other natives, Christian boys, and those wishing to become Christians, were received as boarders into a school, under Mr. Elton's son, and a girls' school, under Miss Butcher, was doing such invaluable work among the girls, that it needed to be at once enlarged. The importance of training up Christian girls so that boys baptised in the schools may not have to marry heathen wives is too well recognised in all mission work to need insisting on.

At the northern point of the island is Kudat where there lives an English Resident and other Europeans. The Mission held here five acres of ground, on which stood a church, parsonage, Chinese deacon's house, mission house, boys' and girls' schools, all completed and paid for. The Chinese deacon, Fong Han Gong, was there. The Rev. R. Richards, their former pastor, visited them from Singapore, and *Mr. Elton went when he could.*

Here the Chinese had been left so long with no resident priest that the German Basel Mission had sent their missionaries, and though all our buildings

St. Michael's Church, Sandakan.

were there, paid for in great part by the people themselves, we are, by our neglect, driving them out from us. As long as Mr. Richards was living among them, the whole population came to church, and all the adults were communicants, but though Fong Han Gong is a man of great power and entire devotion to his flock, he had been unable to cope with the work single-handed.

On the west coast Jesselton had its parsonage and school and a considerable sum of money in hand for a church. Thirty white people lived here and a goodly number of Christian Chinese who begged for a priest.

The climate is beautiful, the people keen, and work abounding. For twenty years Mr. Elton had been writing home of the needs of British North Borneo and *still no one had gone.*

It seems a mockery that Labuan, for sixty years a Crown Colony, and the island which gives its name to the diocese, should have no clergyman for its forty white residents, and its population of miners and others, though here, too, church and schools were ready.

In the hills, almost in the centre of British North Borneo, there was a tribe of some 10,000 Muruts to whom Mr. Edney and Mr. Perry went. The mission house and school which the people built were empty, for Kaningau had had no missionary for seven years. For some time the first Christian prayer in Murut went up from those black boys led by their teacher, " Lord Jesus, give us help, teach us," and now those voices are dumb ; not that the Lord of the harvest did not hear, but that the hearts through which He would work were deaf.

In a book dealing with mission work in Borneo it would be unfair to omit reference to the work other than that of our own Church.

The Roman Catholic Missions, which are under the auspices of St. Joseph's College at Mill Hill, have a large staff, including some seventeen sisters. In Kuching they have large buildings, and a large estate which they are developing on keen commercial lines. They seem to have almost unlimited funds, and so are able to give a good education to their pupils at a price quite impossible for the Church of England, which cannot provide either teachers or material for the purpose in such a poor, starved diocese as that of Labuan.

It may be a cause of wonder sometimes that the Roman Catholics have not accomplished a great deal more than appears, considering the advantages they have had over the Church.

The work of the " R.C. Mission," as it is generally called, is often praised by Europeans in Sarawak to the discredit of the " S.P.G. Mission," even by those who are at least nominally Anglicans, and who seem to be unconscious of the fact that they have any responsibility in the matter. This is part of the general apathy of the Church of England, which is the cause of so much failure and the despair of keen men. If our own people would but loyally support the work of the Church in England and in the mission field, they would have less reason for the invidious comparisons they too often make.

The American Methodist Episcopal Mission has a station on the river Rejang, where their work is amongst immigrant Chinese who were already under their influence in China.

We have noticed above the work of the Basel Missionary Society at Kudat, in British North Borneo, chiefly confined to Chinese. If we had had a sufficient staff this work would never have been begun, and the whole congregation would have belonged to the Church. When we neglected them they sought help from those they had known in China.

The Church of England in Borneo, or as it may be more aptly called "Eklisia Borneo," had been at work in Sarawak thirty years before any Christian work was seriously undertaken by others. If the Church at home had nursed this infant daughter with care she might have been a strong healthy child to-day, whereas she has been so neglected and so left without help that one almost despairs of her life.

It may be imagined that some of the expressions used above are exaggerated, and that we have painted the picture in too lurid colours; but this is not so by any means. It is impossible to exaggerate, and if our readers could but go and see for themselves they would readily admit this. Not that this implies any reflection on those who have gone before. The work done by the three first bishops is simply falling to pieces because there are no men to keep it going.

The first Synod of the diocese met under Bishop McDougall at Kuching in 1864. Since that date the meetings have been continued at intervals. To-day there are practically no clergy to summon to a Synod.

We may quote the words of the present Bishop: "Thirty years ago, when the area of operations covered by the Mission was about half what it is now, there were twice as many clergy".

Those who have worked on through the weary years have done their best, fighting against terrible odds. The fault is not with them, but with the Church at home, which has left them "overweighted, undermanned and fit to founder".

These are but bare facts concerning that fertile island, rich in its wondrous wealth of produce above

INTERIOR, ST. JOHN'S CHURCH, MERDANG.

ground and below, brought by a marvellous Providence under English influence, contributing for us so many articles of commerce and of luxury, and yielding to England so much wealth. Have we no care? Is the Church at home still going to leave the men there to fight against overpowering odds, because each man is trying to do the work of three? Is she still going to send a general without an army, and with but scant supplies? or will she at last realise *their* needs, realise *her* privilege? Will she, ere it be too late, rise to her responsibility? Shall the Church of our northern land stretch forth her hands to that far-off southern isle, so close to the Equator, where she *should* be so close to God, under the light of the Southern Cross, yet with so many hundreds of thousands of her people unknowing of the light of the Cross of Christ? Shall not the North and the South join hands, that so, by prayer and help, to us may be vouchsafed some share in bringing in the glory of those many tribes, that they may be His in that day when the Lord makes up His jewels?

QUESTIONS ON CHAPTER VII

1. Who is the present Bishop, and has he special fitness for his task?

2. Mention what you know of the work on which he has already been engaged.

3. How many clergy are working (*a*) in Sarawak, (*b*) in British North Borneo?

4. Do the natives show any response to the efforts made on their behalf?

5. How does the missionary visit the several missions in his care?

6. What has been the chief cause of the weakness of the Church's work?

7. When was the first Synod held? Why can one not be held now?

8. What is the impression left upon us after reading this story of the crying needs and miserable response?

CHAPTER VIII

Response of the Church at Home

THE last chapter dealt with the present position of the Church in Borneo, its tremendous need, its appalling lack of men.

What is going to be the response of the Church at home to the call? Is it a call less urgent than that of the man of Macedonia to St. Paul in his vision at Troas, calling him on to the West? A West all unknown, full of dangers, of persecution from alien governments, full of perils by land and sea; a West of unexplored lands, of uncivilised peoples, and uncertain welcomes. Yet for him there was no hesitation. The man of Macedonia, whether St. Luke himself, as Sir William Ramsay suggests, or another, stood for the nations behind him; their mythology had failed and had proved to be but vanity; they were in darkness, and he cried "Come over and help us".

And so we read, in one of those wonderful touches of St. Luke's vividness, "immediately" they started for Macedonia; they loosed from

Troas and came with a *straight course* to Samothracia. St. Paul, St. Luke, St. Timothy, Silas, they *pressed on* to carry the good tidings; no holding back and leaving Philippi to wait, even though stripes and imprisonment awaited them there. The door was open, the call had come and they must go.

Now there is the call back. We stand in the isles of the sea, and gaze towards the East. The Empires of Greece and Rome, which prepared the way for the Gospel to be brought to us, have passed away; their glory has crumbled into dust, and the Empire of Britain girdling the earth now has her day. Why should the little northern island wield her sway over millions East and West? Will our Empire, too, crumble into dust? Greece left the world her legacy of culture in literature and art, Rome her legacy of law and order, will England leave her mark only of occupation for commerce, or will she be blessed by nations yet unborn in that she carried the lamp of the Gospel afar?

And as we look and listen, right round the globe comes the voice again, "Come over and help us". Yet how different the circumstances! From the East not the West, from a country known, to a great extent explored, and where the inhabitants are more or less civilised, from a land governed by our own countryman, where there is no fear of persecution, for English rule secures order and safety; but like the call of long ago in this, that out of *their* darkness the people are pleading that we will bring them light.

The response which the Church at home will make is *the measure of what our Faith is to us.*

If our religion is to us the revelation of a higher and more blessed Faith, and if we believe that the Dyaks are as dear to His heart as we are, then we must yearn to bring those wild branches to be grafted into the true Vine, to give them the joy of the knowledge of His love, and when we hear their cry we cannot shut our ears and leave it unanswered.

The Bishops in Borneo have for so long laboured on, trying to grapple with the work of the unwieldy diocese, and forbearing to leave it and come back to stir up the Church in England, that we have some slight excuse, perhaps, for the past, in that we did not know. Evil " is wrought as much by want of thought as want of heart ". But now the need in Borneo has been brought to our knowledge; we *know* at last and we must *do* or the responsibility rests on us. We cannot let the courage and the faith in which the Bishop has gone out be crushed under a hopeless task, nor let him and his clergy feel paralysed by the overwhelming attempt to do the impossible.

First, and above all, must come the prayers at

home. In the words of the Bishop's commissaries: "We want to rally round the Bishop such a bodyguard of praying friends that he will be able to think of nothing but the volume of prayer and sympathy and help that is already gathering behind him here in England. We want him and his little band of devoted fellow-workers to feel that they have many friends at home who believe as firmly and loyally as they do themselves, that in spite of all the difficulties, even though they were tenfold greater, they are well able to go up and possess the good land in the name of Christ, and that they can depend upon those friends to do all in their power by prayer and almsgiving, and every other appointed means, to enable them to do so. 'Not by might, nor by power, but by My Spirit, saith the Lord.'"

It has been said "We need to learn that for the advancement of the Kingdom of God prayer will do more than preaching. Pleading with God for men will do more than pleading for God with men."

"Ye that are the Lord's remembrancers take ye no rest," or "Keep not silence". He knows the needs far better than we, and yet in some mysterious way it is our prayers which bring forth the blessing.

An American missionary, working in Eastern Equatorial Africa, wrote: "My experience abroad has brought me to the conclusion that the saint of

God at home who labours with us on his knees is doing really more for the spread of the Kingdom of God in the hearts of men even than many of us who are occupying posts as missionaries abroad. One is not very long in the mission field before one realises the fact that it is a hard spiritual fight we are fighting, and that behind the evil heathen customs, which are to many eyes harmless, there is a personality, and when we missionaries attack the seemingly innocent customs we find that we wake up the forces of the evil one, showing that the whole design of it was an organisation to divert men from the truth by giving them customs which occupy their minds and much of their time. We need, then, strong spiritual forces in the work abroad to give us the necessary wisdom for our work as well as to dispel the dense darkness which enshrouds the minds of the people amongst whom we work, so that I claim the Lord's work is more hindered by lack of prayer than it is even by lack of funds."

What a veritable agony then of remorse should be ours to feel that by our neglect of prayer we are not only not helping, but are actually dragging back, the work of those in the field, that we are like the "people of the land" who weakened the hands of the Jews in building up the temple. What a tremendous thought that we, even the weakest, may yet be fellow-workers; what an honour that by our prayers we may be permitted to help on the work of God, to strengthen the hearts which are weary, that when some danger threatens or some difficulty looms large it may be lightened because "some one was praying at home". Such a thought must send us to our knees like Daniel three times a day to add to our other prayers earnest intercession for the work in the whole mission field, and most specially for Borneo, in the words of the beautiful prayers drawn up for the diocese, for the Bishop and his fellow-labourers and for the Association at home. This is the first charge laid upon us, and we must not betray our trust.

Our prayers must be for the whole work, laying it all before God, and asking that He will give just what is needed, and then, in particular, for men and means.

How is it that for two months the Bishop made his appeals, all through England and part of Ireland, for men, and yet went out alone? How is it that the younger clergy can be content to stay at home? Even on a lower ground, do the romance and fascination of Borneo which inspired Rajah Brooke make no call to the men of England now, and still more on the higher ground, is there no true romance in being pioneers of the Church, in laying down foundations, in building up the waste places, work which needs the deepest wisdom, perception and

GATHERING PEPPER.

MENGATAL.
(British North Borneo.)

tact? Why is there no response? Are we content to say: "We have sent Borneo a good Bishop, and that is enough; it is nothing to us that the clergy, who have so patiently for years gone on doing their best in their multiplied districts and who looked with eager hope that from 'home' men would come out with the Bishop, were to have their hopes dashed to the ground. It is nothing to us that when the Bishop arrived he was to feel the disheartenment of saying to the people in the vacant stations: 'There was no one in all our great country who would come to you'; that he was to feel the care of thousands committed to his charge, for whom he can do nothing, because alone he cannot reach them, and no men have gone; that he is to go on waiting, waiting, mail by mail, hoping each will bring offers of service and yet none come, even of the eighteen needed to keep up the work already begun, let alone the new fields white unto harvest?"

The Bishop of Bombay, speaking of what a serious effort on the part of the Church to evangelise the world would cost, has said: "It would cost the reduction of the staff of clergy all round. It would cost the laity time and personal service. It would cost some people the difference between a larger house and a smaller one, and others, that between frequent holidays and rare holidays, and so on through all the comforts and pleasures of life.

It would mean the marks of suffering all over the Church. It would mean everywhere the savour of death, and what we have not yet faced, death as a Church, renunciation of spiritual privileges and delights. I call upon the Church to lay down its life in some real sense for the missionary cause." At present we let those who go out lay down their lives from the overstrain, while we sit at home and enjoy our spiritual luxuries.

It is easy to say there are 6,000 Christians, and we reckon one clergyman for a parish of 2,000 in England, therefore three should suffice for Borneo. Picture the conditions, villages far apart up the rivers, scattered in the jungle and on the hills, to be reached only by paddled boats or by dangerous paths. Under present conditions a missionary has to travel for three days to reach some of his most distant villages. If he stays a week in one village how far can he teach the untrained minds about the things of heaven, of which the very meaning of the terms used must be explained to them? The facts for which their faith is asked must be patiently gone over and over as absolutely strange ideas. The love of God! a new conception—that He wants them to love Him and to be good, and that He should have died for them—still more wonderful! Only in the evenings can the people be gathered together, for they are busy outside through the daylight hours.

And after a week the "tuan" must go away, rowing or walking to the next village, and these people are left alone to remember what they can of this strange new hope, till, months after, it may be, the missionary comes again, and then he may find that the people have chosen distant farming land for that year's crop, and are scattered about the jungle living in little palm-leaf huts. They need some one to live near them and teach them patiently day by day. But even to approach this ideal, a small army of native workers is needed, and a sufficient European staff to keep them under constant guidance and influence.

What will they think, those wistful Sarebas, who, when the Bishop's boat is seen coming up their river, will crowd down to the banks and wade out into the water to clasp his hand and to welcome him, when he has to tell them "Yes, I have come, but I have no one to leave with you when I must go away"? How can they think that England is a Christian country? So many millions there, all Christians, and not one to go to them! Christians in name, but in practice put to shame by Mohammedans.

And so we must pray that Bishop and clergy may not have the sickness of hope deferred, and that God will put it into the hearts of the best men to offer themselves for Borneo, and that the way may be made clear for them.

he had recently consulted, showed that out of five million sterling given every year in England and America for missionary work, the Anglican Church contributed much less than one million, and of the money subscribed in England for foreign missions considerably less than one-half came from the Church of England. America contributed more than England, and of the sum which was given in America less than one-thirteenth was given by the Anglican Church. Of ordained missionaries in heathen lands only about one-seventh were, according to the paper in question, Anglican, and of native clergy, only about one-tenth. He mentioned these facts because it was a call to Church people to remember how inadequately they were bearing the part which they ought to bear in the common Christian endeavour to evangelise the world."

Look where we may the Roman Church is in the forefront. She has no lack of priests, of teaching brothers and sisters, of nurses, to go wherever they are needed (and this is especially true in Sarawak).

Among the Moravians one in every fifty-eight communicants is a missionary. In the Church of England Year Book for 1909 the number of our communicants in 1908 is given as 2,142,039; the returns in this book are professedly not quite complete, so that the actual number should be rather more than less, but taking the number given, a proportion equal to the Moravian would mean that we should have 37,114 missionaries. In the same year the European workers, ordained and lay, men and women, supported by S.P.G. and C.M.S.—were 2,122.

Is it not cause for deep shame that this should be the proportion sent out by the State Church of the greatest Empire in the world? Will her candlestick be removed like that of the Church of Carthage because she has failed to carry the Message?

Prayer then should be ours that men and women now may hear and respond to the missionary call, that the homes of England may become missionary centres where the spirit of vocation shall be instilled and fostered, that the quest of money and of ease may give place to the quest of God's service, and that the disgrace of the Church may be averted, for with the disgrace of the Church at home, is linked the peril of the Church abroad.

The native Christians and the heathen stand out in the attractiveness of their character and the picturesque romance of their life, but there must be an appeal to many hearts at home for our own countrymen, for the fine young Englishmen who, in the service of the Rajah or of the Company, are not only introducing modern civilisation, but also standing for English justice—young fellows from cultured English homes, who have gone out with all the excitement of life in a new country before them, and then have come the long days and months and years, often of dreary isolation in the jungle, far from other white men, and the depression and temptations which such isolation brings. They, too, need the means of grace, need a straight word from the "padre" now and then to encourage them to stand firm in the Christian upbringing which it is too easy to forget, and to help them to keep bright their witness for Christ in the heathen darkness around them.

And after our prayers for men must come prayers for means.

To sum up, after carefully weighing the facts the Bishop estimates the needs thus :—

"If the waste places are to be built and the work for which the Church is responsible is to be consolidated there must be three things :—

> More Workers
> More Money
> More Prayer

The mission work that can be done, and the extension that it may be possible to undertake, will depend entirely on the response made to the appeal."

As a minimum and simply to "keep things going" there should be :—

1. *Workers*

For *Sarawak* six priests and nine laymen, or twelve priests and three laymen. There are six mission stations with houses and churches already built, now mostly given over to the ants and the bats. And round about these stations there are Christians crying out for the Word and Sacraments. Two men are needed for each station; it is unfair to leave a man alone in the isolation of the jungle, and the jungle of Sarawak is no place for a married man with wife and children. The clergy, like the Government officers, should be unmarried men, but they must not be left to live alone, therefore twelve men at least are wanted. There are many ways in which laymen, too, could render excellent service: they could give such teaching as is necessary in the schools, and help in ambulance work; there is a great and most interesting work waiting to be done also in superintending the Mission estates, which must be developed by the industry of converts, and valuable industrial work should be carried on in teaching natives to make better use of the jungle. Mere theologians or students, whether lay or cleric, would not be happy in Borneo; the men needed are strong, zealous, sensible men of action, full of sympathy and in the very highest sense of the word Christian gentlemen.

St. Thomas' Boys' School, Kuching.

For *North Borneo* there should be two if not three more priests to minister chiefly to Europeans, though they would at the same time find many opportunities of mission work among the heathen.

For *Kudat* there should be a priest able to speak a Chinese dialect or dialects.

This plea takes no account of work among women, of the extension of our schools in the jungle or of sorely needed medical work.

2. *Money*

A sum of £10,000 should be spent on necessary buildings including repairs, and a sum of £1,000 on developing the Mission estate.

The amount may seem very large, but to spend less the Bishop considers will be unsound finance, a kind of penny-wise and pound-foolish policy which will entail the appeal for more money at no distant date.

Then there would be the maintenance of the new workers asked for; this would come to £2,000 a year, and if the services of the catechists are to be retained their stipends must be increased.

Living in Borneo is enormously expensive and prices are rising rapidly. It is said by old residents that the cost of living has increased by fifty per cent. in the past fifteen years.

For many reasons it would be well if the work

could be organised on community lines. A Borneo Brotherhood is a development continually prayed for, but a religious order cannot be made to order. Every such "order" has come from the devotion of some man or woman whose heart God has touched. We pray that some priest in England may feel that Divine touch and go out to give his life for this poor neglected diocese; he would be warmly welcomed by white and brown alike.

3. *Prayer*

To end as we began. It is obvious that if the Church is to make any effective advance she must depend not on the might of numbers, not on the power of money, but on the Spirit of God. Neither men nor money will be forthcoming without prayer, and without prayer neither men nor money will avail.

Some of our readers may like to use the Intercession paper drawn up for the Diocese[1] as an effective way of rendering real help.

The special funds which are in more immediate need of help are:—

1. The Girls' School and Bishop's House Fund.
2. The Boat Fund. To provide a proper launch for the Bishop, and boats for mission stations on or near the rivers.

---

[1] To be obtained from Mrs. Woolcott, Trinity House, E.

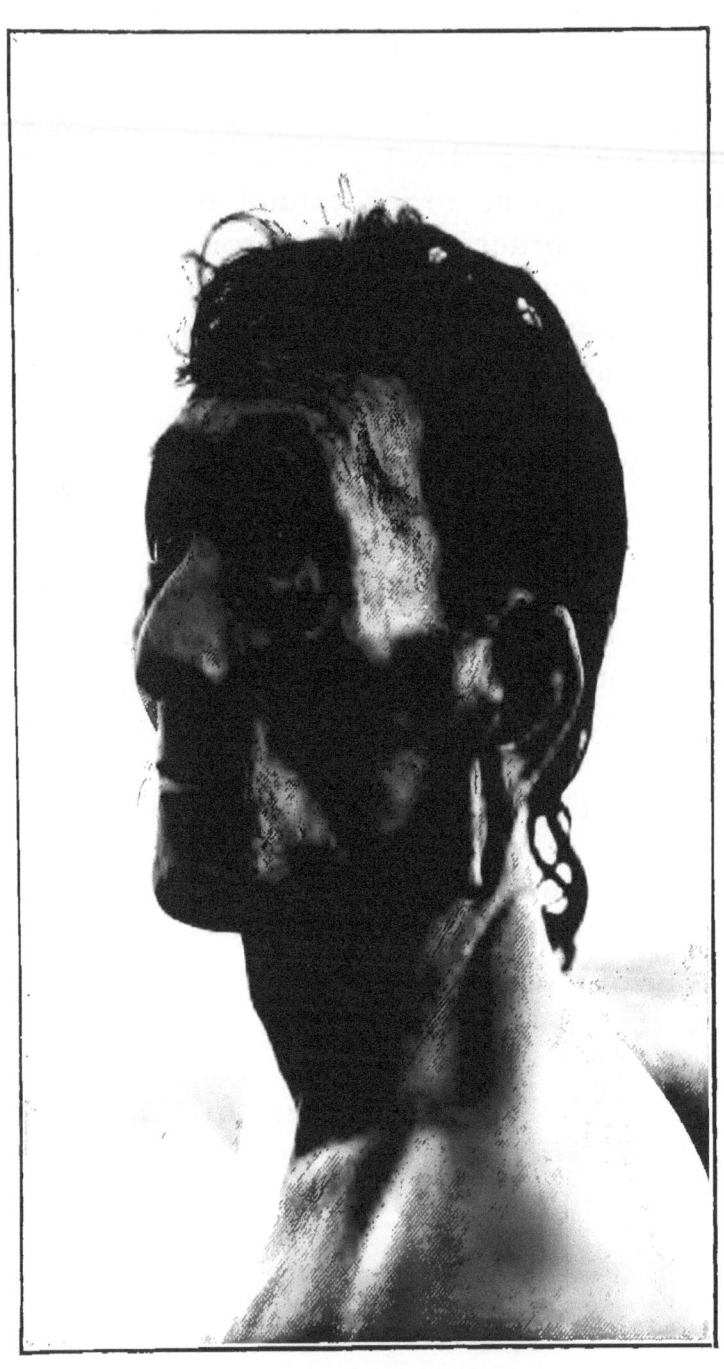

ABAN DENG, A LONG WAT CHIEF.

3. The Bishopric Endowment Fund. At present the certain income of the Bishop is only £270, for the rest he is dependent on annual grants which may at any time cease. Legacies will be given to this Fund.

Draft form of bequest: "I give and bequeath to the Society for the Propagation of the Gospel in Foreign Parts the sum of £   free of legacy duty, which I direct to be paid out of such part of my personal estate as by law I can charge therewith for charitable purposes, to be applied to Church purposes in the Diocese of Labuan and Sarawak, and the receipt of a Treasurer of the Society shall be a sufficient discharge for the same".

The Rajah helps the educational work of the Mission by grants to the schools, but except for this the whole expenses, as mentioned before, have hitherto been defrayed by S.P.G. (save the £270 of the Bishop's stipend). If the work is extended as the Bishop hopes, the S.P.G. grant must be largely increased or supplemented by other help.

To bring all those interested in the diocese into corporate union, Dr. Mounsey, as we saw above, established the Borneo Missionary Association, in connection with S.P.G., that by prayer and gifts the members might take their share in the work. (See page 167 for list of officers.) The Hon. Secretary will be glad to receive help in kind or to send boxes and cards for collecting small sums. Schools and families can defray the entire cost of educating a boy or girl in the Mission at a charge of £6 per annum, and in this way help to train the missionaries of the future.

Friends of the diocese can give no better help than by undertaking to act as "Local Correspondents" for the Association.

What is going to be the response of the Church at home?

"The harvest truly is plenteous, but the labourers are few. Pray ye therefore the Lord of the harvest."

QUESTIONS ON CHAPTER VIII

1. Is there any parallel between the famous cry of the man of Macedonia (Acts xvi. 9) and the cry from Borneo to-day?

2. Why should we not leave the Malays, Chinese, Dyaks, to their old faiths and ways?

3. Can we plead ignorance?

4. What response can we make?

5. What evidence can you give as to the value of prayer for foreign missions?

6. How does the Bishop of Bombay estimate the cost to us of seriously and thoroughly preaching the Gospel to the whole world?

7. Why are more workers imperatively needed by Bishop Mounsey?

8. How can women at home help to gain more workers?

9. What statement was made lately by the Archbishop of Canterbury as to the relative position of Church of England missions?

10. Is it the natives in the diocese alone whom we are neglecting?

APPENDIX

OUTLINE THOUGHTS

CHAPTER I

Borneo and its Riches. — To consider the wealth of beauty and of natural resources, and to look on them as a call to win the wealth of human life, too, for Christ.

a. The geographical position of Sarawak and of British North Borneo.
b. Their natural history.
c. Their inhabitants and commercial products.
d. Our indebtedness.

CHAPTER II

The People and their Customs.—To consider the various races, their need of one ideal as a bond of union, and what contribution each might bring to the Church of Christ.

a. The special characteristics of the three races of human life—Malay, Chinese, Dyaks.
b. The daily life of the Dyaks.
c. The reasons why each race is worth working for, to bring to Christ.

CHAPTER III

Feuds, War and Death.—To consider the people now in a state like that of the Old Testament age, and the call to bring them into the new life of love.
  a. The Dyak at war with his fellows.
  b. The Dyak treatment of sick and dead.
  c. The contrast between such lives and those of Christian believers.

CHAPTER IV

Superstitions and Beliefs, and their Effects.—To consider the deep darkness in which the people live and the suffering caused by their bondage to evil spirits.
  a. The Dyaks' sense of the supernatural.
  b. Their ideas upon sin and prayer.
  c. Their belief in malignant spirits.
  d. Their bondage to omens.
  e. Our compassion.

CHAPTER V

Influence of History.—To bring out how our position of protection is a call to send the light of the Gospel.
  a. The past history of Borneo so far as it touches upon and leads up to our present responsibility.
  b. The life-work of Rajah Brooke.
  c. The response of Sarawak to his efforts.
  d. The gifts which are greater than settled government and justice.

APPENDIX

CHAPTER VI

Sixty Years of Missions.—To help to realise how much has been done and yet how much is still left undone.
   a. Home response.
   b. The work already begun and carried on.
   c. The difficulties to be overcome.
   d. The saddest part of the story.

CHAPTER VII

Position of the Church in Borneo Now.—To consider how past indifference at home has paralysed the work of the Church in this far outpost.
   a. Native response to missionary efforts.
   b. The forces at work under the Bishop's direction, their total inadequacy for the task.
   c. The cause of such under-staffing.

CHAPTER VIII

Response of the Church at Home.—To try and secure an adequate response to the call of Borneo by fresh efforts now.
   a. Fresh efforts or retreat. Why is retreat impossible?
   b. The value of prayer.
   c. The need for genuine self-sacrifice.
   d. The part that women at home can take in this matter.
   e. Our personal response to our own English people, as well as natives, calling to us and waiting.

Names of Clergy Working in the Diocese of Labuan and Sarawak, 1910

The Bishop:

THE RIGHT REV.

WILLIAM ROBERT MOUNSEY, D.D.

The Archdeacon of Sarawak:

THE VENERABLE A. F. SHARP, Kuching.

Allen, Rev. G. Dexter	Banting (in England)
Elton, Rev. W. H.	Sandakan
Howell, Rev. W.	Sabu
Weighill, Rev. W. E.	——
Ah Luk, Rev. Chung	Quop
Han Gong, Rev. Fong	Kudat

Lay Missionaries

Mr. Pierpoint Meadows   St. Thomas' School, Kuching
Mr. A. Elton . . . Boys' School, Sandakan
Mr. Lyon . . . Engineer and Catechist
23 Native Teachers, 27 Lay Readers

Women Workers

[1] Mrs. G. Dexter Allen, M.B. London   In England
Miss Bristowe . . . . „ „
Miss Butcher . . . . . Sandakan
Miss S. A. Kendrick . . . Kuching
[2] Miss C. B. Sharp . . . . „
Miss Olver . . . . . „

    [1] Hon. missionary.   [2] Associated missionary.

List of Mission Stations

Name of Station.	No. of Out-stations.	Missionary in Charge.
SARAWAK—		
Kuching	14	Ven. Archdeacon Sharp
Quop	1	Rev. Chung Ah Luk
Lundu	1	Vacant
Banting	1	Vacant
Sabu (Undop)	9	Rev. W. Howell
Skerang	0	Vacant
Sarebas	20	Vacant
Krian	4	Vacant
LABUAN, with JESSELTON, etc.		Vacant
BRITISH NORTH BORNEO—		
Sandakan		Rev. W. H. Elton
Kudat		Rev. Fong Han Gong (Deacon)
		No European missionary

Diocese of Labuan and Sarawak

BORNEO MISSIONARY ASSOCIATION

(in connection with S.P.G.)

President: THE LORD BISHOP OF LABUAN AND SARAWAK.

Vice-Presidents:

THE LORD BISHOP OF LONDON
," ,, ROCHESTER
,, ,, ISLINGTON
,, ,, KENSINGTON
BISHOP HOSE

Chairman of Committee: THE BISHOP OF ISLINGTON.

Bishop's Commissaries:

Rev. W. G. CAMERON, All Saints' Vicarage, Clapton, N.E.
Rev. R. FAIRFAX SCOTT, Hanworth Rectory, Middlesex.

OBJECT OF THE ASSOCIATION

To assist the work of the Church in the Diocese of Labuan and Sarawak—
1. By the development of sympathy and interest on behalf of the Diocese in such ways as are found possible.
2. By intercession, corporate and individual, for the work and the workers.

3. By raising funds, general and special, for the support of the work.

Members Undertake

To subscribe not less than 2s. 6d. annually, which entitles them to receive *The Chronicle* free each quarter.

To help in some of the ways mentioned in the leaflet " How to Help ".

Honorary Officers of the Association

Treasurer—Rev. W. G. Cameron, All Saints' Vicarage, Clapton, N.E.

Secretary — Miss Turner, Stainforth House, Clapton Common, N.E.

Editor—O. G. Petersen, Esq., 4 Westwood Park, Forest Hill, S.E.

Special Departments

Intercession and prayer—Mrs. Woolcott, Trinity House, E,

Medical work—Mrs. Mosse, St. Paul's Rectory, Covent Garden.

Literature—Miss Eda Green, 1A Sheffield Terrace, Kensington.

Newspapers and magazines (sending abroad)—Miss Hose, 58 Elsham Road, Kensington.

Church embroidery—Miss K. G. Harvest, 57 Fitzjohn's Avenue, Hampstead.
Miss Ethel Truman, Home of the Epiphany Truro.

Collecting boxes and cards } J. Sharp, Esq., 113 The Grove, Wandsworth.
Lantern slides

APPENDIX

Local Correspondents

Berwick-on-Tweed	Miss A. D. Robertson, Ravensdown.
Cricklewood	Mrs. Brown, 188 Fordwych Road.
Hampstead	Miss K. G. Harvest, 57 Fitzjohn's Avenue.
Ilford	Miss Honchin, Cranbrook Street.
Kensington	Miss Hilda Chappel, 3 Sheffield Terrace, W.
Oxford	Mrs. Skrine, The Vicarage, St. Peters-in-the-East.
Penarth	Mrs. Brodie-Butleigh, Clinton Road.
Walsall	Miss Thomas, 50 Elmers Grove Road.
Wednesbury	Mrs. Knowles, Tamworth.
Willenhall	Miss Winnie Hartill, Manor House.

Addresses of Missionaries

Missionaries working in Sarawak should be addressed thus :—

To..

....

       Sarawak,
        Via Singapore.

The word "Borneo" on the envelope will delay the letter for several days.

Missionaries working in North Borneo should be addressed :—

To..

....

       British North Borneo.

N.B.—*British* North Borneo.

ABERDEEN : THE UNIVERSITY PRESS

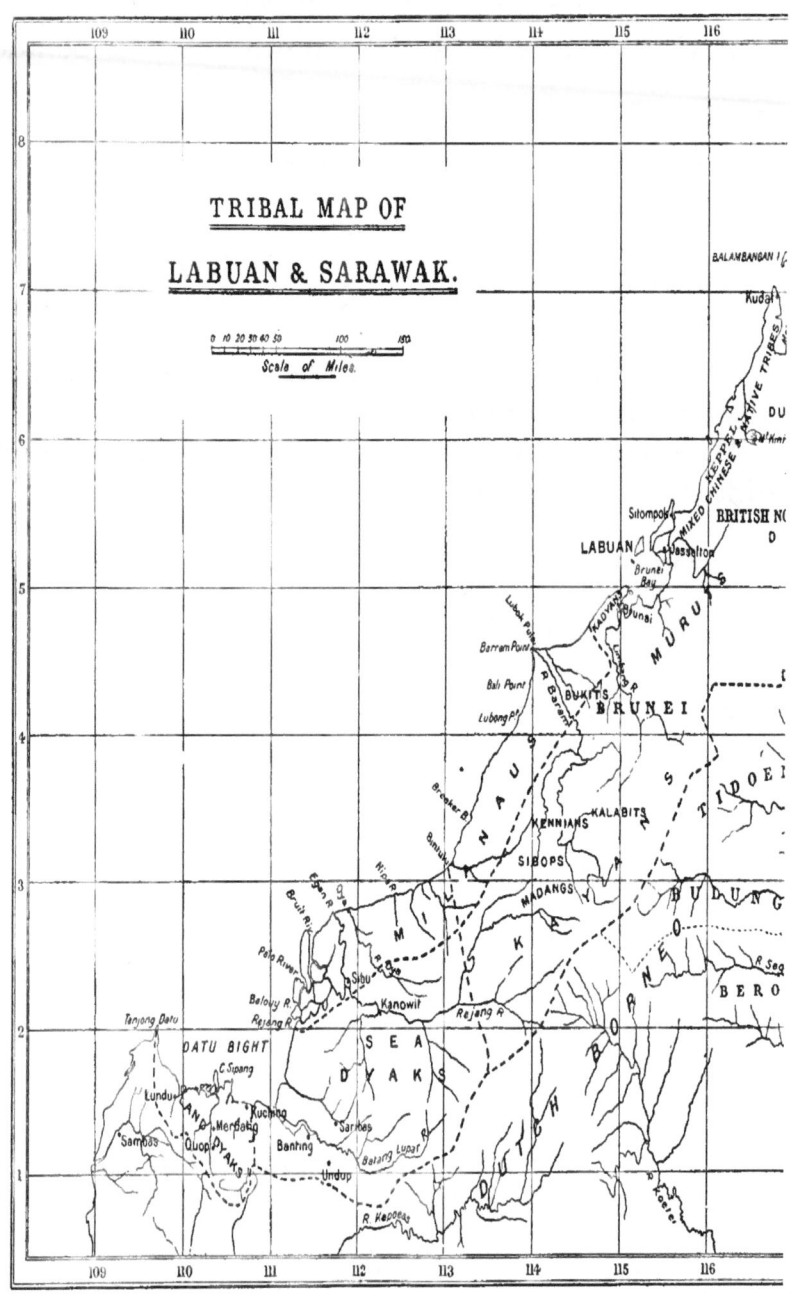

ImTheStory.com

Personalized Classic Books in many genre's

Unique gift for kids, partners, friends, colleagues

Customize:
- Character Names
- Upload your own front/back cover images (optional)
- Inscribe a personal message/dedication on the inside page (optional)

Customize many titles Including
- Alice in Wonderland
- Romeo and Juliet
- The Wizard of Oz
- A Christmas Carol
- Dracula
- Dr. Jekyll & Mr. Hyde
- And more...

WS - #0162 - 170225 - C0 - 229/152/17 - PB - 9781313201506 - Gloss Lamination